wow!

—{ idea }—

that's a

———————————{ opportunity }———————

great

! { action }——————————————

idea!

HOW TO FIND MILLION-DOLLAR IDEAS...AND KEEP FINDING THEM!
CREATE YOUR OWN IDEA FACTORY

Perspectives　　Australia　•　New Zealand　•　Canada

Wow! That's a great idea!
How to find million-dollar ideas and keep finding them.
Written by Ed Bernacki

Perspectives

Published by Perspectives,
GPO Box 1074J, Melbourne, Victoria Australia 3001
Web site www.ideafactory.com.au Email wow@ideafactory.com.au

Edited by Sally Macmillan.
Book design by Nicole Melbourne.
Illustrations by Christina Miesen.
Printed by Australian Print Group.

The National Library of Australia
Cataloguing in Publication entry:

Bernacki Ed,
Wow! That's a great idea! How to find million-dollar ideas and keep finding them.
Create your own Idea Factory.

Includes Index
ISBN 0 646 41224 8
1. Creative ability in business. 2. Success in business.
I. Title
685.4

For information on ordering additional copies of this handbook for business innovation, email wow@ideafactory.com.au or write to Perspectives, GPO Box 1074J, Melbourne, Australia 3001.

About Ed Bernacki

Ed Bernacki started the Idea Factory concept in 1996 to create a greater sense of urgency for businesses to be more innovative. He recognised that too many companies talked about being innovative but did nothing to make it happen.

All organisations need an "Idea Factory" to produce new ideas and new thinking, much like traditional R&D departments did in manufacturing companies. If not, where should new thinking happen in our many service organisations?

Ed Bernacki is a speaker, writer and adviser on the use of innovation and creativity in business. He is also a professional brainstormer who helps companies solve difficult challenges. He leads a company that works with businesses and not-for-profits to identify new opportunities using the tools and ideas in this book. He has published many articles on creativity and innovation in the UK, USA, Canada, Australia and New Zealand.

He also co-created the Conference Navigator Guide called *Wow! That's a great idea!* This unique conference creativity guide was first used by Inc. Magazine in the USA to help people find more ideas at its conferences. George Gendron, editor of Inc. Magazine, wrote about the Conference Navigator Guides, "Once in a while a new idea surfaces that makes me wonder: Why didn't I think of that?"

Ed Bernacki brings new insights and ideas to his writing. After reading this book, if you do not believe the Idea Factory concepts are useful, email him at wow@ideafactory.com.au and tell him why to get a full refund!

For more articles and information on creativity and innovation see www.ideafactory.com.au

Dedication

Finding great ideas is important. But nothing happens if you don't act on your great ideas. Innovation only happens if you act on your ideas!

Thanks to everyone who provided encouragement and support in the development of this book, particularly my parents in Canada, Irene and Paul Reeve Newson, who were always there when I needed them.

Also, to people such as Jim Hainey in New Zealand, who pushed me to commit myself to speak out about what I believed to be important, and the many supporters who saw value in finding new ideas, including Elmar Tomie of New Zealand Post who demonstrated the wisdom to support my initiative, George Gendron, the Editor-in-Chief of Inc. Magazine who shared his insights and supported the use of the Conference Navigator Guides, and Suzanne Merritt, co-founder of the Polaroid Corporation Creativity Lab and co-editor of the Conference Navigator Guides.

Lastly, thanks to those workshop and conference participants who had the courage to try some of the processes in this book to look for their own great ideas.

Ed Bernacki

Wow! That's a great idea!

How to read this book

It's a fact: 90 per cent of buyers of business books do not get past the first chapter. If you are only going to read one chapter, start with Chapter 9. It provides the nuts and bolts of putting together a strategy for making a business more innovative.

Many ideas already exist in our organisations but few of our organisations have the systems or processes to find them, develop them and act on them. Part One provides key insights for shaping a more innovative service-focused business; one that continually solves problems and creates opportunities by finding new ideas when and where they are needed.

Innovative organisations continually outperform their competitors. Creating a more innovative organisation starts by re-evaluating how we make decisions in organisations. People inside our organisations make decisions every day that impact the future. The latest research of the factors that make innovative organisations innovative reveals one key secret—if ideas are important, people need to know how to manage them.

Key to finding new ideas is the desire to do so. Many staff attitude surveys find that a common staff complaint is, *Our bosses do not listen to us*. The result is that they turn off and stop contributing. Start to actively listen to these ideas and discover the wealth that already exists.

3. Where to look for million-dollar ideas!   **29**

There are three approaches that successful businesses use to find new ideas for opportunities for growth. These drive their everyday thinking to replace mediocrity with innovative services, products and processes.

4. Putting the Idea Factory to work   **47**

People must be actively involved with the search for new ideas. Here is the approach to use to maximise the success of the efforts to be more innovative. Consider the Idea Factory to be the equivalent of an R&D department for service organisations.

Part two: The innovative thinkers' tool kit to achieve results   **61**

Here is a series of tools and challenges that can focus the initiative of people to achieve specific results. This Idea Factory Tool Kit has been proven through workshop experience to create solutions to problems or to identify new opportunities. Some help to find ideas, some help to enhance existing ideas and others help you to act on these ideas.

5. The Idea Factory tool kit   **62**

Part three: Earning the title of being an innovative company   **93**

The pathway to earning the title of being an innovative business is to provide the tools, resources and the right environment that tells everyone, *We are open to new ideas and new thinking.* You cannot buy this success. You must create it.

6. Getting to a result   **94**

You must get results to add to the bottom line. Hard results lead to profits. Soft results build teamwork, leadership and your ability to innovate. They are equally important.

7. It's not working very well: troubleshooting the Idea Factory

Troubleshooting the innovation process is crucial. The quality of ideas may be poor or the quantity of ideas may be minimal. Here are top tips to get you through the difficult periods.

8. Building your Idea Factory: a place for innovative thinking

The Idea Factory may be virtual (a meeting room you use for the day) or a full-time facility dedicated to find new ideas. Many companies now have a full time creativity and innovation centre much like a company gymnasium. Here's how to set up an innovation lab.

9. Creating your strategy for innovation

If innovation is so important, why do so few companies set goals to make innovation happen? Add a section to your yearly business plan to include the problems you need to solve, the opportunities you need to create and the process to do both efficiently and effectively.

10. Give credit to the source of your growth: people

Innovative organisations recognise that their strength is the people inside the business. They combine the best efforts of individuals with the collective resources of the organisations to achieve results. Create a business that is open to new ideas, one in which people can actually contribute to the success of the company.

Appendix: Innovation strategy framework

In the future, all strategic plans will include a section for "innovation" to focus on new ideas to stamp out mediocrity and shape new opportunities. Here is a framework for an idea-management driven innovation strategy to make your organisation more innovative.

Why the focus on being innovative?

Inside every company you will find a place where creative thinking happens or once happened. People who started the business knew the value of a good idea. Ideas represented the potential to earn the next dollar. They knew that they had to act quickly to take advantage of opportunities. Often they made decisions without the full facts. They harnessed their experience and expertise to make a decision to act.

The main idea in this book is that the only long-term strategy for business growth is the need to apply innovative thinking to solve problems and create new opportunities.

To ensure that we focus on both objectives, the Idea Factory creates a framework for a company innovation strategy. This is not a technology strategy. It is a strategy with a dual focus of tackling the problems within a business that waste resources and shaping opportunities that create new resources. There are only three steps to shape an innovative business:

1. Learn to manage ideas well inside the business.
2. Create an environment that is open to new ideas and thinking.
3. Provide the leadership and direction to focus this innovation potential on what counts most to the success of the business.

The secret of innovation

With a working innovation strategy in place you create a tremendous company asset. Rosabeth Moss Kanter, the former editor of the *Harvard Business Review* said, "The secret of innovation is that it gives you a temporary monopoly. It means that you can charge more for it."

The monopoly you create is your ability to continually find the big ideas that count. When you do so, you create an advantage that is unique to your company. That's a pretty good reason to be more innovative.

In the future, every company will add an innovation strategy to their business plans just as they do for marketing, operations and HR. After all, if we claim that innovation is truly important, why do we not plan for it?

How to get the most from this book

As people who work with ideas, we must develop new skills to find insights and ideas from conferences, workshops, books and magazines. Here are some ideas for getting more useful ideas from this book.

Pick any chapter to start. Read a section and interpret how it could apply to you or your business, and make a decision to act. *Wow!* was designed to prompt you to find insights and ideas. As you move through the book, summarise your insights at the end of each chapter, using these icons to help you manage your ideas:

Wow! is for the great ideas that just make sense right away. Note anything that immediately seems obvious that encourages you to act.

WOW!

Questions—Notice what intrigues you but requires more information. What questions come to mind?

?

Quotes—Note any statements that you want to repeat at a meeting. You can use a line from the book to start a conversation with someone.

"
"

Actions—What surprises you as a good idea that deserves immediate action? There is power and conviction in moving quickly on a great idea.

a

At the end of each chapter, summarise your thoughts and capture the key insights and ideas.

Remember that innovation only happens when we act on our ideas!

Ed Bernacki

creating business

growth

through ideas

and innovation

part one

1 new
ideas from
innovative
thinking

You know a great idea when you see one. Your customers know a great idea when they see one. Your staff know a great idea when they see one. Exactly what is a great idea? How do you find a great idea?

How can you tell the difference between a good idea and a great idea?

To describe a great idea is somewhat like talking about quality or love—you know when you feel it or see it but how do you measure it or define it? Rather than trying to be too specific, consider this definition. A good idea is simply one of the flashes of the obvious when we see something and say, "Why didn't I think of that? It's so obvious!"

Perhaps one of the most frustrating experiences in business happens when you recognise how easy it would have been to fix a problem had you thought of it. Similarly, how easy it would have been to create an opportunity had you noticed it sooner.

Most people have stories that fit into both categories. The most unfortunate stories involve a customer who took their business elsewhere when some small and trivial problem became too much for the customer to accept.

Sometimes market research can help a business to find these problems before it is too late. A research exercise for a large professional services firm uncovered a fact that was quite a surprise to the senior partners. Most assumed that the quality of their advice was the critical factor in the relationship with the client. In fact, a significant issue was invoicing. Many of the invoices were simply worded,

invoice for services

fees for services
rendered in May   **$8000**

These invoices were often mailed a month or two after the work was finished. The research found that clients assumed quality would be high. The problem that clients had was that they could not remember the work that occurred months ago.

The solution was simple. Add some explanation to the invoice (or add a short covering letter) to outline the project, the work that was done, and the value or benefit that had been provided to the client. In essence, turn the invoice into a management report. In this way the problem was solved before it become an issue. Clients want value for money. The same principle applies for auto repairs, office cleaning, or virtually any service. Customers or clients should always have the option to raise the issue of cost without feeling intimidated.

When you finally become aware of the situation and examine it, the problem starts to define itself. Finding a solution to a problem is fairly straightforward once you recognise that there is a problem. Once the problem is defined, you can look for options to fix it. As you then narrow down the options, based on costs, benefits or any other criteria, quite often the "ideal" solution starts to appear.

By narrowing down your focus, you can identify the key steps that you need to follow to solve the problem. With this in place, you can create that "to do" list of tasks necessary to fix the problem.

A key to successful problem-solving for any organisation is understanding the role of decision-making in business. Decision-making is one of the most important skills for every manager in every organisation. Much of the creativity work is aimed at improving people's ability to make decisions on important issues by instilling a sense of discipline into the decision-making process. Creativity tools and techniques help to:

1. Better define the issue or challenge at hand.
2. Expand the search for options that could satisfy the issue or challenge (including the option of "doing nothing").
3. Enhance the potential benefits of each option.
4. Improve the selection process to find the most beneficial option while building consensus and conviction around the decision.

This sounds rather obvious. Your decisions have a tremendous impact on an organisation. Management writer and researcher Bernard Bass compiled an extensive review of research on decision-making in organisations and found a number of common factors across many industries and cultures. His findings have very little to say that is positive about the quality and ability of management to make decisions in the best long-term interests of the organisations that they work for. Some of the common findings are: we have a tendency to focus on problems, pay attention to the boss, take the easy route, and fall in line with the status quo. This hardly supports innovative thinking.

Pick a handful of decisions and see how many of these observations you can find in your own decisions.

In general, decision-makers in organisations:

- Are slower to react to opportunities than to the alarm bells of problems.
- Pay more attention to superiors than to subordinates.
- Often pick the first alternative that minimally meets the standards of acceptability.
- Make decisions that tend to support other people within the organisation.

How did you rate yourself? The first conclusion is perhaps one of the most troublesome for business. We are reactive to problems but not proactive in getting something right the first time.

Creativity in business in context

Innovation programs and the use of ideas seem like modern concepts but let's put them in historical context. Recognising that decision-making in business is less than optimum is certainly not new.

In 1938, Alex Osborn introduced a process to help teams of people in his advertising agency to use their "brain to storm" through a problem. He later published a highly successful book called *Applied Imagination* on this process. (Reprinted by the Creative Education Foundation.)

The original purposes of brainstorming were:

---------------------------------{ definitions }

Creativity – reflects the processes that result in generating something "new" or original or unique.

Innovation – is the process of generating something new and viable that adds "value" to an individual, organisation or society.

- To improve the quality of decision-making in group meetings by getting people to contribute their ideas.
- To improve communication within the teams of people.

Osborn saw that too much time was wasted in meetings that produced few new ideas. This original definition is as relevant today as it was then. In time he modified his model for brainstorming to focus on three phases: fact finding, idea finding and solution finding.

At about the same time, the American government realised it had to improve its industrial capacity to supply the war effort. To achieve this goal, a national consulting service was set up to work with industry to improve its effectiveness in delivering the many products needed to supply American soldiers overseas. This was greatly complicated when America entered the war and many of its skilled employees enlisted. This loss of skilled management and labour created a tremendous pressure on the many factories across the country—a pressure that proved too great for many organisations.

The consulting approach was soon abandoned. It was not able to deliver systematic results across the country. It would have been impossible for a small army of consultants to work with thousands of companies that needed to enhance their effectiveness. This led to the investigation of the potential for a national training program to work with the people in those businesses.

A program called "Training Within Industries" was created to maximise America's production. It was a train-the-trainer program designed to train a set of managers whose skills would cascade across the company, and eventually the country. It was this multiplier effect that was missing with the traditional consulting approach.

"Training Within Industries" focused on three areas and targeted supervisors and management, who were seen as the major inhibitors of productivity. The three areas were:

- **Job Instruction Training,** which taught supervisors the importance of proper training for the workforce and how to provide the training.
- **Job Methods Training,** which taught how to generate and implement ideas for continuous improvement.
- **Job Relations Training,** which taught leadership and human relations.

The structure for this program was very powerful and is as relevant today as it was 60 years ago. It could be the latest theory on managing knowledge workers. Why do we not recognise the value of these more subjective areas in today's business schools? An underlying theme throughout the program is that every employee is capable of finding new and better ways to do their job. The program also emphasised that employees should never stop thinking about improvements that can be made.

In the reviews of the "Training Within Industries" program some impressive results were discovered. These included:

- 86 per cent of companies reported an increase in production of at least 25 per cent.
- 100 per cent of the companies reported that training time had decreased by 25 per cent.
- 86 per cent of the companies reported labour hours reduced by 25 per cent.
- 55 per cent of the companies reported that scrap was reduced by 25 per cent.

- 100 per cent of the companies reported that grievances had been reduced by at least 25 per cent.

In his review of the program, Alan Robinson, author of *Corporate Creativity*, (published by Berrett-Koehler, ISBN: 1576750493) quoted this paragraph from a letter sent by a company president who had been involved with "Training Within Industries".

> *"Under no circumstances do I want you to make public my name or that of my company. While I want you to know what this program has done for us, still I must not have it known to some of my stockholders who would immediately ask, 'What have you, Mr President, been doing all these years to overlook such a possible reduction in expenses which would have meant increased dividends to us?'"*

"Training Within Industries" was built on the premise that we recognise the importance of leaders in business who can lead by maximising the contribution of employees. They provide people with the skills they need, recognise the value of the ideas employees contribute to the success of the organisation, and provide the direction and understanding necessary to lead a diverse group of people.

After the war, these principles were not forgotten. The biggest threat to America at the time was seen to be a devastated Japan. The industrial output of Japan fell to 10 per cent of its pre-war days. The threat to America was that Japan would look to Communism as the way to rebuild the country. To ensure that this would not happen, the Americans thought it would be useful to train the new managers as Japan had lost much of its pre-war workforce. The model of "Training Within Industries" was exported to Japan and over the next 25 years, vast numbers of Japanese managers were trained to deliver these principles within their organisations. As a result, thousands of companies and millions of employees learned how to find and manage ideas that led to improvements.

The idea for creating a factory to find ideas

We are generally good at solving problems when we want to solve them. There are many books and training programs written on this topic that can help you understand the process of solving problems. We are far less skilled at developing the opportunities that we face. Why? Opportunities are almost the reverse of a problem. They are harder to identify. They tend to have many options. As such, it is harder to focus on an opportunity. It is hard to research an opportunity. People have a very hard time of giving you comments on something that does not yet exist.

Imagine spending a lot of money to develop glue only to find that it barely sticks to paper. For most of us, such a situation is one of those problems that you want to sweep under the carpet. For 3M, it led to the idea of Post It Notes. It went on to become a multi-million dollar idea. Have you ever considered how many other companies may have developed similar ineffective glue and wrote off the investment as a failure? Or have you ever considered how a company could have put in place a process to come up with new ideas that could have led to the opportunity for Post It Notes and the need for a glue that barely sticks?

Every one of us has torn up bits of paper to use as bookmarks. We have all folded a page to help us find our way back to that spot. However, none of us came up with the Post It Note, and yet it is so blatantly obvious!

The Idea Factory came out of direct experience with many organisations in North America, Australia and New Zealand. They were a mixture of entrepreneurial not-for-profit organisations, very staid professional service organisations, and for-profit businesses that make you wonder how they survive in business. Some were small while others had thousands of employees. The degree of interest in innovative thinking and new ideas had little to do with size, profit motive, complexity or structure. It was more to do with attitude. You can summarise much management research on leadership, training and organisation development and suggest that businesses fall into one of two categories:

1. Those that welcome new creative ideas, learn from them, are not scared of the changes that new ideas may require, and are led by people who are not threatened by those who find new or better ways to do things.
2. Those that do not welcome ideas or new ways of thinking about the organisation.

As an ideas person, experiencing a product, an event or a service has often made me wonder, "If they only added this option, it would be so much better!" Other ideas people find that it is better to hide their ability within the corporate world as they quickly learn that people with ideas are often thought of as being troublemakers, complainers or too ambitious. The reaction they meet is, "What's wrong with the way we do it? It's worked for us in the past! If you don't like the way we do it…"

With that, ideas people learn to ignore the creative spark and settle down to a life of frustration in a mediocre organisation. In reality, many managers who have uttered such creativity-killer criticisms actually meant, "I'm the boss. It's my job to think. I can't have someone else, particularly a junior, make me look bad!"

There are books written on the creativity-killer lines in business. How many of these do you recognise?

- We've tried that before!
- It'll never work.
- There's no budget for anything new.
- It'll be more trouble than it's worth.
- We've always done it this way.

The list could go on for pages. Ultimately, many ideas people develop stories, which go this way: "I thought of that last year, months before our competitors came out with the same thing. If only they had listened to me."

A study in New Zealand looked at the most critical issues hindering inno-

American CHIC THOMPSON, a creativity writer and consultant, listed many creativity-killer phrases in his book, "Yes, But…" His definition:

Killer Phrase 1. A knee-jerk response that squelches new ideas; most commonly said by bosses, parents and government officials. 2. A threat to innovation.

vation in business. These results are certainly not limited to any one country. How many do you recognise from your organisation? The key factors hindering innovation were found to be:

- Creative people are squashed or controlled.
- The incentives for "champions" are low.
- The emphasis for compensation is short term.
- Top management takes a short-term perspective.
- Mergers rather than innovation drive growth strategies.
- A strong influence of accountants and lawyers who try to control companies.
- There is a high personal risk of failure for innovative people.
- There are limited incentives for "intrapreneurs" (those inside an organisation).
- Centralised decision-making often does not allow for variation.
- Management's reluctance to invest in real training.

As a test of your business, ask your staff to comment on these findings. Their responses may surprise you.

The concept of the Idea Factory

The Idea Factory does not have walls or any other fixed assets. The only cost may be coffee and sandwiches to fuel the people involved with generating ideas.

The Idea Factory is a series of processes and tools designed to generate a continuous source of new ideas. If this sounds appealing, then you are set to tackle the competition and prepare for the future. If you think it is wasted management time, start looking for a new career. You may not be in business in 2010. Though forecasts vary tremendously, the vast majority of today's companies will not operate under their existing structures in 10 years time. This reality is vastly more complicated by the Internet. The ability to link customers locally or globally can produce new business ideas and revenue sources that were not even imaginable a decade ago.

Here's what the Idea Factory system is:

The Idea Factory is a business innovation strategy stressing **ideas and knowledge** as a competitive edge. It is based on two observations:

1. Many "good" business ideas already exist in the minds of staff, suppliers or customers but they remain buried. At best, managers don't ask staff or customers for ideas. At worst, the corporate

culture kills any innovative streaks the staff may have had within weeks of joining the company.

2. Few businesses use a system to access the knowledge that exists within the organisation or to enhance it further. In some cases, good ideas happen despite the "system" rather than because of it.

The Idea Factory is a system for developing ideas and results (not just training) and building them into your day-to-day plans. As with any factory, there are certain requirements. For example:

- You need raw materials such as a challenge to focus on, a commitment to the process, time, creative energy, background information and personal preparation.
- You need to "process" the raw materials in ways that add value to the organisation. This is your machinery for brainstorming from new or different perspectives, which often leads to new insights and ideas.
- You need to ship a result out the door to get a value and ultimately business growth. For example, you develop an action plan, start a new service or improve customer service in specific ways.

As with any factory, it can be used as needed. You can do it by yourself, with a small team of staff or in combination with some outsiders to get that special perspective.

The Idea Factory is a step-by-step process to teach business how to find ideas and develop these into profitable results. The process can focus on a challenge to:

- Develop business opportunities.
- Solve business problems.
- Manage issues critical for your future success.

Many companies already undertake some form of idea factory within their business. Whatever we call it, a well-conceived "idea" strategy will always help a company to achieve better results, for one simple reason. If you harness the creative energy of people— from secretaries and night watchmen to the CEO and customers —and focus them on specific challenges, a mix of intuition and experience combines to produce good ideas. Someone may have a "part" idea. Someone else adds another concept before a third adds the final piece to the puzzle. Suddenly a fourth looks at the overall situation and sees the total idea—the solution to the challenge.

Though it seems mysterious, it's how good ideas happen. Sometimes brainstorming workshops go nowhere until someone sees something, which then triggers the entire group. For the next hour ideas can fly through the room. Many of these ideas will have dollar signs attached to them. Those who regularly work with the tools of creativity and innovation will have seen many big ideas worth a lot of money being created.

Suzanne Merritt co-founded the Polaroid Creativity Lab in Cambridge, Massachusetts. As well as training employees of the company in problem-solving and creativity techniques, the Lab was used to stimulate creative thinking throughout the company. It was reported that the Lab is credited with created solutions for problems and ideas or concepts for new products worth in excess of $US30 million. The consulting firm PriceWaterhouseCoopers found a powerful link between innovative thinking and profits when it studied the factors that help UK-based organisations innovate. It later surveyed 800 companies in various countries. The message the survey delivered was simple yet sophisticated.

According to the author of the survey Trevor Davis, the biggest surprise was that "there was such a close relationship between innovation and financial performance. We found that those major companies that were generating more than 80 per cent turnover from new products and services at least doubled their market capitalisation over a five year period". The 300 companies studied were large multinationals, part of the Times 1000, including Gerber Foods, IBM, Johnson & Johnson, Nike, The Post Office, Bayer and Shell Research.

To translate the survey findings into insights, the conclusions from this study on the long-term profitability of a business are:

- **The only way to do better than a competitor is by doing something noticeably different.**
- **The ability to innovate, learn and change is the hallmark of lasting corporate success.**

The survey looked at the factors that hinder or enhance the capability for innovation. It looked at factors relating to an organisation's ability to implement new ideas. Much of the focus was on launching new products and services but the research found a strong correlation between those companies that continually commercialise new ideas and the ability to also focus ideas on internal systems and processes. The very top companies apply new ideas anywhere and anytime, be it to conceptualise new products or to enhance internal processes.

It also dealt with some myths, such as that certain industries are more innovative than others. Some people mistakenly think that technology and innovation are linked. They may be. Innovation may be technologically driven. R&D may be driven by technology but what drives the scientists to be inquisitive, curious and creative so they find new, unique or original solutions to challenges? These are people management issues.

PriceWaterhouseCoopers found that top performers could turn over their whole product and service portfolio every five years and innovate broadly across the entire business. How do they achieve this?

The most innovative businesses make innovation a priority at board level, releasing risk capital whenever and wherever it is needed to support bold ideas. They continually examine where they should focus innovation efforts for maximum benefit and are passionate about what they do and how they do it.

The survey reveals the 10 characteristics that separate the highest performers from the lowest, with trust as the number one differentiator. These 10 factors are grouped together as three underlying capabilities. Each is worth noting:

1. Idea management processes

These high performers focus on developing critical underlying capabilities that underpin their success and distance them from the competition. The top 20 per cent in the survey turn their ideas into action via well-defined idea management processes which:

- Seek ideas and knowledge widely from customers, suppliers, employees, other industries and competitors.
- Allow ideas and knowledge captured to be shared, stored in user-friendly form and made freely accessible.
- Actively encourage diversity of viewpoint, talent and expertise.

- Delay the premature evaluation of new ideas by giving managers considerable discretion to pursue ideas without subjecting them to a formal appraisal.

2. Shaping a creative climate

The most innovative companies bring their idea management processes to life by creating a climate that encourages ideas to flow freely through the business by:

- Developing and promoting people who share a common set of values and using both values and competence as criteria for appraisals.
- Using carefully designed reward and recognition systems to reinforce management behaviour that encourages innovation.
- Training managers to support as well as challenge and to coach rather than direct so that they create a climate more favourable to innovation.

3. Balancing leadership and delegation

An effective balance between leaders and followers is crucial to sustaining an innovative working environment. For the highest performers this means:

- Defining which decisions can be taken unilaterally and which must be based on consensus, so that the social contract between leaders and followers is made explicit.
- Recognising and rewarding people who take the lead in encouraging others to challenge current ways of working by, for example, sponsoring and protecting mavericks.
- Employing human resource processes, which, by recognising that leadership roles are often separate from management positions, selectively promote role models at all levels of the organisation.

PriceWaterhouseCoopers' important global review of innovation concluded with the powerful realisation that, "Successful growth will come from those businesses that harness all of their people in the elusive pursuit of future market needs. We are leaving behind a period in which new ideas were associated exclusively with individuals (like a corporate Einstein), or specialist functional departments such as R&D or Marketing. Now we recognise the importance of involving all levels of management and employees in business innovation.

"The poor performers were in effect like portfolio managers putting all their money into one company called R&D and praying that a single big idea would come through. The successful performers were spreading their bets across a much wider range of companies called brand, process, shop floor, office workers, distribution and others, as well as R&D, to produce results. In the opposite of what would be expected, where risk brings rewards, it was the high risk takers who were under-performing and the ones adopting a more conservative, inclusive approach who gained benefits.

"In high performing companies, innovation has become a corporate-wide habit, where anyone can come forward with an idea and expect to be at least considered seriously. In certain industries, the flow of fresh thinking is encouraged by its structure. Employees in these sectors are seen less as permanent staff and more as free-lancers contracted to complete specific projects. Once they have done so, they move to solve new problems with new employees."

To focus on managing ideas and creating a climate open to new ideas almost seems at odds to the focus of so many business schools and management text books. In company after company, the most profitable were those that managed the "soft issues" as they are often referred to; the people issues and the skills that people have to create value. Yet we rarely teach these valuable skills.

Starting the process to harness ideas

Though it has few costs, the Idea Factory and all innovation processes must be fuelled with these resources.

Energy and enthusiasm are necessary to sell the concept of an "idea factory" to your organisation. When you are trying to introduce something new, nothing is more contagious than energy and enthusiasm. However, staff and managers may be cynical about any new program. Too many fads have come and gone.

Time is the key raw material. People must have time to think, ask questions, and talk to customers or others important to the issue. Years ago, a university professor gave me some valuable advice when he suggested that the biggest challenge you have is getting time to put your feet up on the desk to think about the things you did that day (more on this later).

Honesty and integrity are necessary to share company information. Hiding information hinders participation. All staff, from the newest recruit to the longest-serving employee, will see through any short-term attempt to take advantage of their ideas. Respect and reward are part of the integral process.

Executive and organisational commitment is necessary to convince everyone that innovative thinking by everyone is important to the organisation's survival and growth.

With the fundamentals in place, you will be guaranteed a return. At minimum, the organisation will be stronger because it can harness its knowledge, experience and expertise. At best, you will find more million-dollar ideas than you can possibly deal with.

Focus on results

Critical to the overall process is defining what you want to achieve from your Idea Factory.

Further practical experience can be gained by attending formal workshops that are driven to create a particular strategy or build a new type of service. These introduce some key concepts and challenge traditional perspectives; you can even arrange some team-building to lubricate the process.

The Idea Factory should only be used when you have defined a "challenge". Consider this to be the first result—a well-defined statement is easy to understand. For example, a customer service challenge could be worded:

> Our company is getting a growing number of complaints from customers telling us that they have problems installing our product. Our challenge is to learn why customers have this perception, why the problem(s) exist and what process and steps we will undertake to satisfy our customers' concerns.

Commit yourself to writing down the problem in terms of specific words and actions. Often this process alone will help you to solve the problem.

The purpose of the challenge statement is to focus everyone involved on the results. The challenge is a one- or two-sentence summary of what you want to achieve. It should outline your understanding of the problem or the potential opportunity or need. The focus on results is critical for two key reasons:

1. A positive result will easily justify the investment in terms of cost of time and resources that are used.
2. A challenge that ends with a good result will be very satisfying for those involved. Success is very motivating. People will feel that the process is worthwhile.

At all times, focus on achieving the result that was set for the session (eg get a key strategy in place along with the key actions necessary to make it work). If you achieve your results, the by-products of the Idea Factory will be fun, team-building and training.

Not every idea session will end with a million-dollar idea. Sometimes you have to recognise other types of important results. To start with, a good result will be to have your team believe that the Idea Factory is worthwhile and worthy of their contribution. Once people become comfortable with the process, results will be more defined and specific. Ultimately, you will find ideas that save you money, ideas that make you money and ideas that protect the long-term value of your business.

Even bad ideas are good

While I completed my MBA at the University of Otago in New Zealand, an opportunity arose to work with New Zealand Post. The postal business was in a state of flux as the former government department had been restructured into a State Owned Enterprise (a business model in which the organisation is expected to show a profit with the government being the sole shareholder).

The project involved a study to conceptualise new ways to deliver mail to the business sector. People in the marketing department, who were busy developing plans to market the numerous postal services, always seemed to be too busy to look at a new concept.

On the last day of the project, the only person left to approach was Elmar Toime then the general manager of marketing. His office was on the executive floor. I thought, rather hopefully, that he could spare five minutes to review the concept. He did listen for five minutes, and he said to continue. Ninety minutes later the meeting ended with an assignment to produce a report on the idea.

Overall he did not think it was practical to implement the idea but he was intrigued and wanted to spend more time with it. What he said always remains with me as a key indicator of the leadership necessary for an innovative culture. He said, "I wish more people would come to me with ideas, even bad ideas, because it means people are thinking."

Several years later, New Zealand Post was awarded the title of Company of the Year by a national business publication and Elmar Toime, by then the chief executive, was selected as the CEO of the Year. After a particularly profitable year, New Zealand Post lowered the cost of all domestic mail by 12 per cent. New Zealand Post has a formal system of studying trends and issues important to its business in the future. It keeps an eye on the impact of technology and change on its markets and services.

Looking back at our meeting, I recognised the value of his comments. If he had used a creativity-killer line like "It will never work", I would have left frustrated and very reluctant to invest my time in thinking up new ideas. His support spoke volumes for his belief in the value of new ideas. His leadership was more important than any formal programs the organisation could create.

To find innovative ideas takes people with the right tools and perspectives. More importantly, it takes the right environment that allows people to think and contribute, and it takes leaders who are prepared to "walk the talk". After all, the best ideas are already inside most companies. We need to create the systems and processes to find, nurture and act on them.

Insights
from Chapter One

- Creativity helps us to make better decisions in business.
- Ideas, no matter how small, that lead to innovative solutions are the seeds of business growth and success.
- Learning to manage ideas and creating a climate open to new thinking is crucial for any organisation to grow and develop.
- Most of the best ideas already exist within a business but few businesses have systems or processes to find, nurture and execute new ideas when and where they are needed.
- The Idea Factory approach provides the insights and tools to allow you to focus your thinking on finding new ideas wherever they are needed.

Convert these insights into **action** for your organisation.

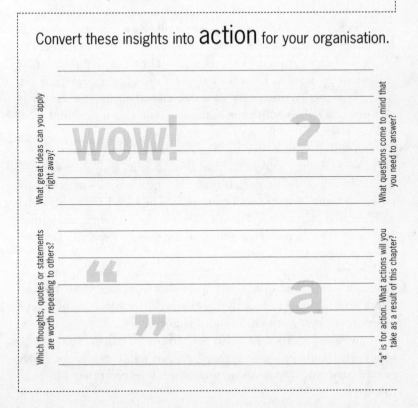

What great ideas can you apply right away?

Which thoughts, quotes or statements are worth repeating to others?

What questions come to mind that you need to answer?

"a" is for action. What actions will you take as a result of this chapter?

2 how to find your ideas!

The thought of an idea factory may seem odd at first. After all, factories are places where things are built. Raw materials come in one door. You use some type of production plan and machinery to create something from the raw materials. Then you ship them to the market to get results. The Idea Factory works in the same way but there are no walls, machinery or warehouses. By using the creativity and ingenuity already in your business, you create a time and place to look at specific problems or opportunities.

You still use raw materials. The raw materials are time to invest in the ideas, energy, experience and your insights and understanding of the business. In manufacturing, the specific raw materials are based on some form of production plan. The Idea Factory also uses a production plan called "The Challenge". The Challenge is a written statement that focuses your time and energy on a specific problem or opportunity to get a result.

You also need a production area (you can use a meeting room, sit around a picnic table or find any space that works for you). You can select from a number of tools to give you different perspectives on a problem while you are inside your "factory".

As with any factory, you also need to ensure that you get a good result. This could be a winning idea, plan or solution. It is absolutely critical that you focus on getting a result every time. More on this later.

Innovation processes like the Idea Factory are business philosophies that separate industry leaders from the followers. Is this too bold a statement? Not at all. When you read the research by the experts, one aspect of forward-thinking companies comes up time after time. It is the ability of these companies to develop products and services that create the "wow" factor; something the consumer had not expected. These companies have the ability to anticipate what consumers want, not just what the consumers need.

Many of our most successful products and services started with someone's intuition. Perhaps the most sensational product launch in recent years that is a result of intuition is the Sony Walkman. Very little traditional market research was undertaken for this product. It is a product that has to be seen to be understood. It would be very hard to imagine the thought of sticking a stereo to the side of your body and walking around with it until you actually see it.

Many of the large multinational corporations have formal procedures for investigating new ideas. They recognise that new ideas are a major contributor to their future earnings. Some large organisations actually target future earnings based on products that have not yet been developed. Smaller businesses can do the same.

The Idea Factory captures the same sense of urgency and importance to be innovative in our thinking. You can use this approach in any situation:

- To focus on a particular customer service problem.
- To create new business opportunities.
- To create a new service, product or process.
- To develop a new strategy to achieve a business goal.
- To develop a new customer service approach, a new service or a new product.

Not-for-profit organisations can use the same approach to solve problems or develop opportunities in exactly the same way. For example:

- Develop a new membership growth strategy for an association.
- Develop an overall approach to generate new merchandising opportunities that add value to the membership.
- Create new fund-raising strategies.

In the future, the issue of whether an organisation is not-for-profit, government sector or for-profit will become rather meaningless to employees. What will count is whether the organisation is innovative or not. By no means does business hold the monopoly on the ability to be innovative in terms of producing value. Innovative organisations will create value for their customers, members or constituents. This will become a greater concern for the educated knowledge workers of the future. Let's start with some definitions:

{ definitions }

Ide'a n. 1. conceived, created, discovered, plan of action; intention. 2. way of thinking, to be ambitious, rebellious.

Fa'ctory n. workshop, buildings and equipment for manufacturing.

Ide'a Fa'ctory n. 1. a set time and place to create good ideas; to explore business problems; to speed business innovation, opportunities and profits. 2. a long-term strategy for success.

Ide'a Fa'ctory Strategy n. 1. a system designed to find ideas to solve problems and develop opportunities on a regular basis using the principles of innovation and creativity. 2. the set of problems to solve and opportunities to create in a given period of time.

This definition for the Idea Factory is not in the dictionaries but it is as relevant as any strategy that you can develop. All businesses have a sales or marketing strategy, a production or service delivery system, an accounting or control system and some type of staff/ human resources strategy. Your strategies look toward the future and help to shape the organisation you want to create.

Why not include an "idea" department that gets together once a week, once a month or whenever you need to come up with good ideas?

The goal of the Idea Factory is very simple. It provides the route you can follow to grow your business through new ways to solve problems and create opportunities. When we do so, we succeed in reaching our objective. Consider:

Succee'd v. to have success, accomplish one's purpose, accomplishment of what was aimed at, attainment of wealth or fame or position, thing or person that turns out well.

A wonderful extension of this definition from the French language is a great theme for anyone trying to capture the true benefit of working for a creative, fun and profitable organisation:

{ definition }

Succes fou (sookas foo') n. success marked by wild enthusiasm.

That's a result that we all want in business.

Put your feet up

One of my most important business lessons came from a university professor. During one of his final lectures before graduation, he said to always "put your feet on the desk for ten minutes to think about what you did that day, why you did it, was it necessary to do, and how could you do it better". He captured so much common sense in one sentence. However, it may take years to recognise the value of this statement to our organisations.

Though it seems to make sense that you should look to improve your performance on a regular basis, too many managers still consider this practice to be non-productive. Far too many employees have learned that they are expected to keep their heads down working rather than thinking. This must change. This is particularly true of professional services whose main "tool" is knowledge, yet they charge for their time based on the number of minutes worked.

Employees, particularly those whose main tool is "knowledge", must be allowed some time to focus on making improvements. Talking and thinking about problems and opportunities adds value to a business. If a modest improvement can be made to something that is required on a day-to-day basis, consider the long-term benefit over a year, two years or more.

Give yourself permission to play

The problem that employees face trying to think applies equally to many business owners and managers. They often say they are too busy dealing with too many problems. However, the same rule applies. Take the time to consider improvements that you can make. Remember the advice…put your feet on the desk for 10 minutes to think about:

- What you did today.
- Why you did it.
- Was it necessary to do?
- How could you do it better?

Another question can be added to this list: What value did you add to the business today?

Idea Factory workshops require a period of time for people to get comfortable with the idea of stepping back to focus on the long-term issues of their business. This shift in focus takes a long-term perspective to balance the short-term day-to-day pressures most people face. The longer-term focus is necessary to continually create opportunities that represent your future earnings.

In essence, the workshop concept gives people permission to take some time to put their feet on the table, to sit back, and appreciate that new ways can be found to add value to the business. They have permission "to play" at business for a few minutes. The results are predictable. Something special happens—an insight is gained, an idea is created or a problem is solved.

An issue for any company encouraging staff to develop ideas is ownership of the ideas and the resulting success. I have seen great ideas created by support staff for which management later took credit. You can take credit for a consultant's ideas (that is what they are paid for). However, think twice before doing this to your employees. If you don't, you may not see another new idea. Integrity and honesty are crucial for innovation. The following golden rules for the Idea Factory provide the perspectives you need to get the most ideas from your organisation.

The golden rules for creating innovative organisations

1. Listen to people

Listen to people when they comment, criticise, offer suggestions or ask questions. Respond positively.

There is a belief that for every customer who complains about your service, another nine stay silent. Do not silence the one who dares to speak up. The same applies for staff who offer ideas. Sometimes it is very hard to keep your composure if someone is complaining. Understand where their anger and frustration is coming from. The best thing you can do is to listen, understand their concerns and thank them for the comments. Don't be patronising or defensive. Many tremendous opportunities have been wasted with comments such as, "What's wrong with the way we do it around here?"

2. Seek out ideas people

Seek out employees, suppliers, customers and others who are ideas people.

Develop networks of people who can contribute a wide variety of perspectives to your business. Look for enthusiastic people who are prepared to think about important issues and make decisions. Employees or customers who challenge the status quo are not the enemy; they are your best allies. They are the source of your new insights and ideas.

3. Respect ideas

Support and respect ideas that are generated. Give credit where and when it is due.

We want to generate ideas that get business results. Not every idea is workable from the start. Be positive and support the initiative. People who make suggestions are taking a personal risk. Sometimes they may not be able to explain it very well. Don't trivialise them. Encourage them.

4. Be committed

Be committed to the process of finding ideas for the ongoing success of your business and its people.

The Idea Factory and all other business strategies that you adopt may end up being "just another fad" if they do not become part of the culture of the organisation. The Idea Factory is designed to produce results that are measurable and tangible. Sometimes the best result may be a better understanding of a particular aspect of the business. Other times it may be a new service that you can launch the next day. From experience, Idea Factories have ended with a plan for a non-profit organisation to earn over $500,000 in the following year. Another ended with simply a commitment and the conviction to complete an implementation plan. Be committed to the process.

5. Give ideas

Give ideas generously to others knowing that you will be rewarded in turn.

If you see an opportunity that a customer, supplier or anyone else could use, take the initiative to tell them. The same applies for problems. Encourage ongoing discussions. At the very least, you may develop a supporter who can refer business to you.

The test for innovation potential

When your organisation develops new policies for human resources, sales, marketing or operations, ensure that they encourage new ideas. Ensure your programs create the right environment to support the people who come up with new ideas. Test your organisation's business decisions and policies. Understand the impact of these decisions on the people in a company who can make a difference to its future profitability and growth.

The Idea Factory

The golden rules for finding ideas in your organisation

1. Listen to people   Listen to people when they comment, criticise, offer suggestions or ask questions. Respond positively.

2. Seek out ideas people   Seek out employees, suppliers, customers and others who are ideas people.

3. Respect ideas   Support and respect ideas that are generated. Give credit where and when it is due.

4. Be committed   Be committed to the process of finding ideas for the ongoing success of your organisation and its people.

5. Give ideas   Give ideas generously to others. You will be rewarded in turn.

 # Insights

from Chapter Two

- ✪ The Idea Factory is a metaphor to describe creativity. The process creates a sense of urgency to solve the problems we face and the opportunity to create.
- ✪ All organisations, including not-for-profit, government or for-profit businesses need innovative thinking.
- ✪ What counts is whether the organisation is innovative as measured by its services, products and processes.
- ✪ Golden rules come from experience and insights. Understand the impact of your decisions on the people who can make a difference to your organisation, and its profitability and growth.

Convert these insights into **action** for your organisation.

What great ideas can you apply right away?

What questions come to mind that you need to answer?

Which thoughts, quotes or statements are worth repeating to others?

"a" is for action. What actions will you take as a result of this chapter?

where
^{to} look for
million-dollar
ideas!

3

The heart of innovation is the ability to see things that do not yet exist. Children are the best at this. They create entire worlds in the clouds or a mud puddle. Artists, writers and designers have a variety of tools that they use to do the same thing—education, travel, or a natural curiosity to understand the world.

So many executives seem to believe that business is rational and definable. Despite thousands of studies on leadership, best practices, strategy, economic conditions and so on, our ability to use this information to create businesses that will be "successful" and "profitable" is still ad hoc.

Too many organisations rely on outsiders for their ideas at the expense of learning how to do it themselves. Outside advisers and consultants should be a resource to use but not the source of your ideas. They can be used to enhance the ideas or help to execute them but the core ideas are best when they come from those who know the business, its customers, suppliers and history.

We can study five, 10 or even 100 businesses to see what they did to be successful. However, this can only tell us what other businesses did under a specific set of conditions. We must resist relying too heavily on such information. It can never reflect the issues facing your future. These studies are useful for providing important issues to consider; but the ideas must come from inside your business.

Basing everything on research is like driving forward in your car by looking at the rear view mirror. You can see where you have been but your focus is not on where you need to go. The findings from customer satisfaction monitors may give you some trends but rarely the insights and the actions that can make the difference.

To go forward, you need to open your eyes to the signs around you and take the time to understand the meaning and implication of what you see. If you see a right-turn sign or a caution sign, you need to react to the road signs or you end up in trouble. If you see a long straight section of road, you can assume the trip will be smoother.

We must be able to read our businesses and our industries in the same way. Much material has been summarised to recommend the following perspectives to help you to understand how ideas are found. Our objective is always to create profitable long-term businesses. Each of these perspectives offers a key to discover something about the organisation that leads to insights and new ideas. The sources of new innovative ideas come from three basic directions:

1. Customer needs versus wants.
2. Changing the rules of the game.
3. The opportunities in opportunity.

To find opportunities, it may be as simple as looking at the mud puddles in new ways. You have to take the time to see what is there! It is important to remember the philosophy of simplicity (or as some say, the KISS Principle—keep it simple, stupid!). The business challenges facing large international businesses are not that different to those facing small organisations. The differences are often to do with scale, not complexity. The secret of creating powerful solutions to problems or to shape new opportunities is to keep it simple, focus on the two or three critical variables most important to the success of the idea and the decisions necessary to make the idea a reality. The complexity gets added into the discussions as you develop strategies and actions. The sharper the focus on the initial idea, the more powerful will be the strategies designed to make it come alive.

Solve problems but remember the opportunities

The Idea Factory is an approach that continually focuses on problems and opportunities that you face in order to tackle the challenges that each represents. The dictionary defines problems this way:

Pro'blem n. difficult task or question, thing hard to understand, arrangement in which one is challenged to accomplish a specific result.

Problems tend to look much harder from a distance. When we can avoid it, a problem is far too challenging to deal with. It is only when the problem becomes immediate, that is, when we are forced to accomplish a specific result, an answer is always found. With the sudden pressure comes the need to find a solution. It may not be the perfect solution but it usually fits the problem. Let's use some examples:

1. The customer is threatening to leave.
2. Your product faces a recall.
3. A competitor is using a new marketing strategy.
4. The parts you need for an order are lost.
5. Three key staff people have announced they are about to leave.

Many short-term solutions can be built into permanent solutions by applying a systematic approach. This simply means considering the problem to be part of a system. That is, if you fix the system, you eliminate the problem. The systems in your business may not be obvious at first. If you prefer, think of the routines that you have to do to order stock, answer telephones, service customers, schedule production and so on. All these activities are systems, which you could set out in a series of steps. Much of the strength of quality accreditation such as ISO standards is that it forces you to consider the systems and document them.

If you notice a problem, it probably arose in the past and may arise again. If you can separate those problems that happen only once and those that repeat, you have already found a key to your solution. The secret is this:

- Match a short-term, one-off problem with a short-term solution.
- Match a long-term, systematic problem with a long-term, permanent solution.

In other words, do not use a bandage when you need a plaster cast. That would be ineffective. Conversely, if you are covering a simple cut, don't use a plaster cast when a bandage would do. That would be highly inefficient. Match the solution to the problem. So often in business, we forget this simple idea and end up applying a short-term solution to a long-term problem. The result is that you end up seeing the problem over and over again. Let's review our problems:

1. The customer is threatening to leave

You have a problem here. By the time a customer threatens to leave, you have already caused damage to the relationship. Something has been annoying them to such a degree that they are prepared to end the relationship. The cruellest aspect of this situation is that you didn't even know it! Your goal is now to understand why the customer perceives there to be a problem, what they would perceive to be an adequate solution, and how you can "make up" for the failure. Also, you must determine how many other customers are in the same situation.

2. Your product faces a recall

Most companies have an emergency or contingency plan already prepared that outlines the important customers, officials and suppliers that must be contacted. Never underestimate the potential for disaster. Not long ago, a 25-year-old Australian food company was ruined in days when it faced a major food contamination problem and failed to respond with integrity. Your recall will get media coverage. Tell the true story. Many companies have managed to turn the negative publicity into positive news by being open and honest.

3. A competitor is using a new marketing strategy

By the time you learn of a competitor's new strategy, it is probably well advanced. As such, the competitor is building momentum. That's your biggest risk. With every success they experience, the bigger the threat they become. Their people will start to enjoy the rewards while you are left wondering what they will do next. In every such situation, decide if this represents an immediate threat to your existing customers or if it will make it much harder to gain new customers. You must also ask why they were able to take advantage of a situation and you weren't.

4. The parts you need for an order are lost

Ranting and raving will not fix the problem. If your parts are lost, it is an operational problem that needs fixing. However, make sure that you focus on the problem and not the symptoms. Don't jump to the conclusion that people are to blame. Look at the systems, too. What will prevent the problems from occurring again?

5. Three key staff people have announced they are about to leave

If your first sign of an internal problem is a resignation letter, then you have lost touch with your organisation. In this case, part of the problem is management and the policies they put in place. The systems that have been put in place for employees are simply inadequate. The issue is rarely money. Most people feel a sense of loyalty to an organisation they feel good about. Money is often the excuse for leaving rather than the cause.

In every case, we must understand the problem and its numerous issues and try to eliminate it. The other significant use for the Idea Factory is to create something totally new: that is, an opportunity.

We use this word "opportunity" in so many ways. We have "golden opportunities" and "windows of opportunity". We know that opportunity only knocks once! I would be willing to bet that for many businesses, a golden opportunity not only knocked once, it knocked a dozen times. It opened the window and walked in yet no-one noticed. Management probably closed the window, not feeling the winds of change blowing through their business and the industry. With that, the opportunity waved goodbye and flew to the competition. Consider the definitions:

{ definitions }

Opportun-ity n. good chance, favourable occurrence.

Opportune a. well-selected and timed, occurring by design.

In combination, consider an opportunity to be a favourable occurrence that is well-selected, well-timed and designed to happen. Many businesses are far better at solving problems than they are at creating opportunities. There are two reasons for this:

1. There is often a sense of urgency for solving problems. Customers are complaining and you need to react. It is an immediate problem and takes over from any long-term planning. We call this "fire fighting".
2. To create something new takes initiative, energy and time; something most organisations perceive that they have little to spare. It also involves risks to challenge the status quo, something most managers want to avoid.

The irony is obvious—when you look closely at businesses that ignore opportunities, had they developed their opportunities the fire fighting may have been avoided by some fire prevention. Secondly, highly innovative companies would not only prevent fires, they would find an opportunity by selling this "fire prevention" to less innovative companies.

To have a problem, something must be in place and have gone wrong. To create an opportunity you need to put something in place and make something happen. That's why it is much harder! Unfortunately, too many businesses spend too much energy cleaning up messes rather than adding value with good long-term ideas. Remember to focus on problems but always invest some time and resources in developing the opportunities.

The lesson is clear. We must create a sense of urgency for creating opportunities that equals the urgency we have to solve our problems.

By finding solutions to our problems we can become more efficient in our operations. However, to be profitable in the long term, we must create new revenue sources and opportunities.

1. Customer needs versus wants

Is there a difference between "needs" and "wants"? It is much easier to talk about and deal with "needs". The reason is simple. Few people, including your customers, can actually clearly tell you what they want. Generally, they will know what they want when they see it, taste it, feel it or experience it. For example, when you walk through a store looking for a special gift, a shop assistant becomes an annoyance when he or she asks if they can help. You will know what you want when you see it. Until then, it is a mystery and very difficult to explain.

The following case study is an example of this. A law firm wanted to understand how their real estate services compared to its competitors. The approach was straightforward. A consultant posed as a prospective client and contacted 15 law firms to ask about their services. Each firm was given the same story—that the prospective customer was new to the city and had to work with a new lawyer.

After seven or eight interviews, a pattern appeared. Most lawyers saw the service as a technical issue; you review the legal contract once an offer is made on a house. In each case, the lawyers provided the service that fulfilled the need—to ensure the contract is workable and legal. However, everything changed with the ninth interview.

When this mid-sized firm was asked whether they provided real estate services, the receptionist responded in a friendly and positive way, and said, "We certainly do, let me put you through to our managing partner."

As the discussion started, the managing partner interrupted the conversation in mid-sentence and advised that nothing be signed until they had met and discussed the options to ensure that the best deal possible was obtained from the bank together with the proper clearances. For the next five minutes he gave ideas and advice and clearly demonstrated he wanted a long-term relationship with his client. Buying a house is the first step. He insisted on sending a letter and an informative checklist he had prepared. This package arrived in two days.

A scale of 1 to 10 was used to rank each of the law firms. But this firm went far beyond addressing the need for legal advice. It also addressed many of the "wants".

- A *"want" to know more about the house buying process.*
- A *"want" to know more about negotiating a good deal on mortgages.*
- A *"want" to know the research that was necessary to check for liens and other city ordinances.*
- A *"want" to learn about wills and other related services.*

The managing partner provided the information in 10 minutes. The cost estimate was consistent with the others. However, his approach and confidence changed the scale of the evaluations. It went to a scale of 1 to 15 to reflect how good he was and how weak all the other businesses were in comparison. By understanding consumers' nervousness and caution involving the biggest purchase of their lives, this law firm set a new standard for service.

This lawyer's systematic approach to dealing with new potential clients was inspiring. He understood what was needed but also understood what was wanted. To maximise the impact on prospective clients, he had developed a number of systems to simplify the delivery of the services. For example, the telephone receptionist knew how to recognise a business opportunity. She knew the services on offer and responded positively.

If you think this is common, take your own survey of the next 10 companies you call regarding a particular service or product. How many receptionists are knowledgeable enough to sell you on a service or product?

The receptionist put through the prospect to a senior person —the founder of the business. The receptionist provided the name of the person in the process, a very nice touch.

His style was informative, polite and enthusiastic. He deferred questions of cost until he had explained their services and the benefit to be received. His cost was competitive.

He took a name and address in order to send a letter. (Of the 15 businesses in this test, only four asked for contact details.)

He followed up with a letter and mailing as promised.

Keep an eye on the future

It is very difficult to assess what people want. With legal services, people need a trustworthy service and want to feel that they received value from the work. However, when someone finds a way to provide their services (which many believe to be quite generic) in such a way as to make people go "wow", then you know they are reaching the "wants" of people. The best way to look at the wants of people is to be an active listener and watcher.

Listen to your customers. Listen to your staff, particularly the young staff as they represent a market you may not understand. Listen to the media. Listen to common sense as the person on the street defines it. Too much time can be spent "doing" business and not enough time spent with people. We begin to lose touch with the subtle changes that are happening. Also, watch how people use your service or product. Watch how they pick it off the shelf. Watch what they do and listen to what they say. You may find that you get two different perspectives. What people say they "want" or "need" may not be what they really want or need.

This is a growing area of research called anthropological research, which is designed to study the behaviours of people. In essence, it is using the techniques that anthropologists use to study modern or ancient societies to look at how people use your product or service. Keep in mind, how people actually use a product or a service which can be very different to how they may talk about it in a focus group or a more traditional research exercise. This style of research is used to make distinctions between what a company or its people say happens in contrast to what actually is happening.

Look for these trends and consider the wants that consumers will create.

- We are getting older as a society, yet we are getting more adventurous with age. People want to walk, hike, experience things and take advantage of their health. Recently, there was a story about a New Zealander who took up bungy jumping and parachuting for the first time at age 86!
- The shift in our age concerns is also creating opportunities that cater to changing the buying habits of the baby boomers who are now turning 50. It is expected that the market for natural

and health foods will greatly expand as more and more people become concerned with age and the quality of their diets.

- The role of women has changed and continues to change in many countries.
- Stress levels are thought to be increasing in many societies.
- Families are getting harder to define but the importance of the family unit is also growing.
- There is a huge change in lifestyles occurring as the boundaries between home, work and recreation merge. Many tradespeople have worked on their own, often from the garage. Today, thousands of home offices exist, with owners picking the times that they want to work and play.
- The environment will continue to be a major focus for people.

These trends reflect people's needs and wants. Writers such as Hugh Mackay, Faith Popcorn, Alvin Toffler and John Naisbitt provide tremendous opportunities to study trends. In addition, many market research companies package industry and "trend" reports which can provide an effective way to keep on top of issues as they are developing.

The best companies today are trying to define the "wants" of their customers. On a global scale, companies such as Sony invest millions in social research to develop an awareness of trends to anticipate what people will "want" in the future. It then builds products to fit these wants. The same applies to all industries, services and products.

Tourism is undergoing just such a radical change. Many people now want to experience something, not just see it. Those innovative companies that are creating opportunities for tourists to get a touch, taste and thrill of the local environment will be the leaders of tomorrow.

2. Changing the rules

Imagine that a new competitor that changes the rules enters your industry. Their hours are longer. They have a different service approach. Their selection of products is better, or they simply work harder at the little things. Even you're impressed with their business. They have had the opportunity to study your business and to determine how they could do it better. They set a new standard for the industry and a new set of industry rules.

This is often the case when a company becomes complacent (or always was complacent) and a new competitor moves in. Rather than fighting to add value to their customers, services or products, they panic, and fight to protect their markets by crushing potential competitors and enhancing the status quo.

Once in a while, we witness a major shift in the way an industry works. What would today's restaurant scene look like without the influence of McDonalds? Would hamburgers be so popular worldwide? Would the entire franchise industry have developed without McDonalds?

McDonalds and the cultural icons it has created, the "golden arches", the Big Mac and the sales pitch, "Would you like fries with that?" have become the new standards in many countries. The company's reputation for quality borders on the excessive. It demands that its ventilation systems prevent cooking smells entering the eating area. It wants systems to work virtually flawlessly. To meet these standards, at least in one country, McDonalds went to a military supplier whose expertise was building sophisticated heating and cooling systems for the Navy. No other supplier could build a system robust enough to meet its standards.

McDonalds did one thing very well. It standardised its entire production system. In the process, *it changed the rules of the game.*

A Canadian grocery company changed the rules for generic no-name or no-frills grocery products that now impacts consumers in many countries. David Nichol of Loblaws recognised that retail discounting was not an effective long-term strategy. He believed that "delivering good and consistent value will inspire loyalty in a way that killer promotions or fantastic prices cannot". He created a line of quality yet competitively priced house brand products called "President's Choice". Throughout the 1980s the line of products grew to more than 1,600 food and related categories. He also created marketing programs that focused on educating and exciting customers rather than simply relying on price discounts.

As the sales of President's Choice products skyrocketed, the concept was packaged and exported to many countries under local names such as "Australia's Choice" and "Sam's Choice". Companies that are trying to catch up to the new rules have also copied it under such names as "Master's Choice" and "First Choice".

President's Choice changed the rules based on the insight that consumers would respond to more innovative products that are presented in interesting ways. Nichol took the focus off price discounting and put it on value and innovation.

In New Zealand, there is a tremendous innovation of changing the rules of the fitness industry. Over a period of 20 years, the members of Les Mills World of Fitness became very demanding users of its various aerobics classes. The gym began to thrive and expand as people found that they enjoyed doing trademarked programs such as PUMP, Body Jam, Step and Supa Circuits. The size and volume of the Auckland-based fitness facility would rival any gym in the United States. Many of its evening fitness classes attract 200 to 300 participants to each of the three aerobic studios. However, this is not the most innovative aspect.

The owners realised that very few gyms have the expertise to develop aerobics classes and to deliver these classes. It realised that there was a tremendous market if it could package the programs and train instructors to deliver the programs. It learned its lessons for marketing and packaging aerobic programs very well indeed. Programs such as PUMP (a cross between weight lifting and aerobics) can now be taken at some 5,000 gyms in the UK, the US, South America, Japan and Australia. For a small gym in a small country, Les Mills changed the rules and now teaches people how to sweat in many different countries.

On a local level, the same revolution can happen by changing the rules. Take-out order windows have moved some restaurants ahead of others as did automatic teller machines in banking. Delivery services for chicken, pizza and even car servicing is also changing the rules in many markets.

Changing the rules is the equivalent to a refusal to play the established game. If someone challenges you to a bike race, you change the rules by zooming ahead on a motorcycle. They get left in a cloud of dust thinking that they were preparing for a cycling race.

Changing the rules of the game is moving from a retail bookstore to offering the same books on the Internet and passing the savings on to customers. These types of virtual stores will change the rules in many retail sectors.

Changing the rules of the game moves a book retailer to offer related "leisure" opportunities such as magazines, compact discs and computer software.

Changing the rules applies for small companies as well as multinationals.

Changing the rules involves looking at every component of your business and seeing how you can reinvent it. How can you make it better by reshaping the way your services or products are delivered, priced and so on?

Changing the rules can also work in consulting. A client was dissatisfied with its previous consultant. It was clear that he did not perceive he got value and he reacted when another offered a guarantee of service. This offer of a guarantee changed the rules in a small way—just enough to win the business. So far, no client has ever requested a refund. Will other consultants begin to offer guarantees? Only the courageous are prepared to live by the perception of the quality of their advice. A common belief among some consultants is that client dissatisfaction usually stems from clients who don't know what they want! Perhaps consulting is another industry ready for a new set of rules.

Changing the rules of the game is a difficult scenario to create. However, all businesses should be aware of the rules and the potential for change to happen. Something as simple as a change in legislation that suddenly allows foreign competition, reduces a tariff or dictates the use of recycled materials will change the rules.

One way to recognise the rules of the industry is to compare your competitor's brochures side by side. Compare how they look. Compare the services and support services. What do they have in common? Is one or more different from the others? How do you compare? Compare the systems for ordering, shipping, replacements and so on. Compare the website. Compare their use of email. Get a sense of the standard way of doing business and find ways to change the rules that add value to the customers, and ultimately your profits.

3. The opportunities in "opportunity"

To create an opportunity, or to innovate, is to take a risk. The risk is that you may fail, or lose money or status within the business. It is often very difficult to measure the benefits of the opportunity in advance of actually undertaking the opportunity. Even the most sophisticated of business plans, forecasts and computer simulations can only stick a flag in the ground and state that your best guess is a benefit of this or that size. There is no certainty. There are no facts. All we can do is to maximise our opportunity.

The "opportunities in opportunity" reflects a belief that beginning the process of innovation opens any organisation to a new potential. Once you expand your organisation's thinking and problem-solving potential, you create an environment in which business is fun and challenging. We all know that there is nothing more satisfying than achieving a challenge. Imagine your employees and colleagues being so fascinated by a challenge that they decide to think about it for the weekend or the evening for the sake of getting a result. This does happen! It is not idealistic nonsense.

If you have never worked for or with an organisation that never stops thinking, do so! They exist and are generally leaders in innovation, job satisfaction, profitability and fun. They have learned how to harness the imagination and passion of the people within the business. Remember the research on decision making quoted earlier: good companies make good decisions.

The "opportunities in opportunity" are the business opportunities that you will create based on your intuition, experience, expertise and common sense. Here is how it works. Assume the typical approach that many companies use for solving a problem is this: they decide that they must fix a problem and settle on the first available solution. Many companies end at this point.

If we consider the "opportunities in opportunity" we would view the problem as an opportunity to finally fix something that is long overdue. As such, it is worthwhile to view the problem broadly to find the efficient and effective solution. Our goal is to maximise our benefits and to never "revisit" the problem. Our motto is, fix it once, fix it right and never see it again!

Instead of accepting the first easy solution, look at the assumptions (eg the established rules) used to define the solution and challenge them. What assumptions have you made regarding the industry, your company, your services and your customers—about the standard rules for the business? Understand these assumptions and you can look at the problem in different ways.

One such case is worthy of note due to its simplicity. The marketing manager of a company had been particularly distressed about the corporate Christmas card. It was simply very dull and projected nothing of value about the company. It was suggested to a director that an option was to commission an artist to produce original artwork for a card that was colourful and exciting.

This idea was planted in the director's mind. He then suggested that the idea be expanded to host a contest for the local Art College. The winner would receive a prize and the art would be used on the card. Suddenly, the idea began to grow into an opportunity as various enhancements were added:

- A local art gallery hosted a two-week public show that generated media coverage for the gallery, the artists and the company.
- Staff were involved in the selection process for the Christmas card.
- An official launch function was held to which clients were invited.
- Most of the paintings were sold, representing the first commission for most students.
- The actual Christmas card highlighted the company's support of art and students. Clients commented that they thought it was a great idea.

This became a regular event, which started from dissatisfaction with a Christmas card. It developed into a tremendous opportunity for very little additional cost. Two principles are at work here:

1. Continually asking, "Is this the best we can do?" in a search to eliminate mediocrity.
2. With this insight, don't stop nurturing and enhancing the initial idea until we have explored the full potential of the concept.

There are many such opportunities around us all the time. Come up with options to solve your problems. If you get stuck, change one of the assumptions. Generally a range of options will be available that each represent a different type of opportunity. Before long you will see that a preferred option floats to the top. This one tends to offer the best opportunity.

Another way to look at this is to use a road map to plan a trip. If you know where you want to go, it is highly likely that a range of routes will take you there. Each will have different costs (time, fuel, tolls, etc) and a number of benefits, such as speed, scenery, comfort, safety and so on. By looking at the assumptions that you used to decide upon your first option, you can then expand your options to consider the other routes you can take based on different objectives. For example, consider the opportunities within this opportunity. Consider:

- The most efficient way may be the expressway—it is the fastest way.
- The most effective way may be the scenic route—as you are preparing yourself for a major presentation and the scenic route puts you in a positive frame of mind.
- The preferred route may combine some of both options.

Again, a solution that combines a range of benefits will float to the top as the preferred option. As already stated, this approach means you must put your feet up on the desk to think about the options. It is important to do so. The notion of "opportunities in opportunity" was refined while working with not-for-profit organisations. Often it was necessary to consider some event or program well in advance to find options or scenarios such as:

- "affordable and do-able" based on existing resources.
- "potentially affordable" if we could find a little extra resource.
- "dreaming and stretching" unless some major support is available.

The planning did not take very long at all. After a while two events kept occurring:

1. In general the organisation had to settle for the "affordable" but saw the potential had it had extra resources.

2. By planning ahead, the seeds of the opportunities were planted in the back of people's minds. Occasionally something that was "dreaming" suddenly became do-able as some critical component suddenly changed. Perhaps funding became available or a particular skill was found with a new employee. The opportunity was quickly built into the plans.

In all cases, opportunities were created from other opportunities. The members of the not-for-profit association became the winners as the association enhanced its services at no further cost. It simply had a vision of a better way, allowed it to grow for several months, and looked for the right factors to make it work. At minimum, this process allows for a better solution than by simply accepting the first option. The "opportunities in opportunity" approach is very powerful.

What we can achieve

The purpose of this chapter was to convince you that you should always be looking for ways to improve the ways we do things. These perspectives are yours to use. When you look at a situation ask yourself:

1. *Are you focusing on immediate problems at the expense of future opportunities?*
2. *Are you satisfying needs or wants? What are the benefits if we start to consider your customer's "wants"?*
3. *Are you simply complying with the industry's rules? What benefit could there be to change one or more? What would the benefits be?*
4. *If you decide to adopt the philosophy that opportunities exist around us, what opportunities will be facing you? What would the organisation need to do on a regular basis to create opportunities?*

These are good perspectives to use as they develop a feeling that you can accomplish something by making it into a challenge. The tools in the following chapter will provide you with some specific techniques you can use to look at your challenges. By using them, you will find new ideas and new ways to be profitable.

Insights
from Chapter Three

✪ Solve the problems but remember the opportunities. We tend to over react to the alarm bells of problems and ignore the silent golden opportunities.

✪ Drive your innovation efforts forward with three broad perspectives. Use these to look for insights that your competitors have missed:

1. Recognise the difference between customer needs versus wants.
2. Make your motto change the rules of the game.
3. Pursue the opportunities in opportunity.

Convert these insights into **action** for your organisation.

What great ideas can you apply right away?

What questions come to mind that you need to answer?

Which thoughts, quotes or statements are worth repeating to others?

"a" is for action. What actions will you take as a result of this chapter?

putting the idea factory to work

Many people use some form of brainstorming workshops to find new ideas. Public relations companies and advertising agencies often find themselves under pressure to find a new creative concept or promotional plan for a client. They react by assembling a team of people to discuss the immediate deadline and the client's needs to find a suitable solution. They meet the deadline with a proposed plan.

Experience in this process clearly suggests that this is not maximising the business opportunities that are available to us. All too often, because of the time pressures, people go back to familiar approaches and recommendations. They end up using the same ideas that were used in the past. To suggest anything outside the "square" is generally thought to be too hard, too risky or too difficult because of the need for an immediate solution.

Every organisation, be it a public company or a not-for-profit charity, understands the need to use quality processes in all aspects of the business. This same "need for quality" is required in our search for new ideas and opportunities.

Finding ideas and opportunities is not a simple and rational approach. You cannot dictate that people start to be creative as if you can turn on some switch. Many reference materials on product development and similar topics view this process as a series of logical steps.

Gifford Pinchot in his book *Intrapreneuring* suggests that it's not simple and straightforward. "Innovations never happen as planned because no one can accurately plan something that is really new!" It may involve intuition or a formal research study. You will hit some dead ends, some mistakes and some problems. However, if you use a "quality" system to support the process of finding ideas, then you can welcome the roadblocks and detours as they lead to a better result in the end. You must learn from these mistakes. Remember that bad ideas can be good if you gain some insight from them. Treat them as opportunities to learn.

The Idea Factory provides the "quality" system. This chapter outlines a series of steps that you can use to start your own Idea Factory workshops. Once you become familiar with the process you can then tailor it to your specific needs. Finding ways to improve the system is the very essence of good innovation. There are three key steps for success of the Idea Factory.

1. Take ownership of the Idea Factory.
2. Define what you want to achieve.
3. Set up a system.

1. Take ownership of the Idea Factory

The only management programs that succeed are those that are driven by the commitment of the people at the top to believe, use and support them. Too many good programs fall into the pile labelled "Another Management Fad" because they were not supported.

No entrepreneur, manager, owner-operator or executive director could argue that great ideas are bad for business. Likewise, who can argue that fitness is bad or cutting back on smoking is bad? The reality is that there is no relationship between how good something is for us and our actions. How many people can honestly say that they have never bought a fitness membership, exercise equipment, a self-help book, a diet program and failed to use it? I suspect most of us have such books and equipment buried in our closets or in the basement.

Though the Idea Factory is simple in its presentation, it will provide many benefits outside of the workshops. Its most important objective is to build your business into a team that works together for the betterment of the organisation and the people in it. That's your long-term vision; a better, more creative, financially profitable organisation. For a not-for-profit organisation, the vision extends to becoming a more effective organisation, one that satisfies your stakeholders and uses your resources efficiently.

The interesting aspect of this approach is that many people within organisations want to contribute. They want to create better job opportunities, to have more security and to have some fun. People enjoy the privilege and respect that is involved with brainstorming and finding new ideas. They will also feel a sense of satisfaction when they achieve a result.

The most effective way to build teams within your organisation is to achieve "results". People relate very strongly to situations in which they participate and contribute to a process that succeeds. Remember back to your sporting successes and the enthusiasm and passion that a positive result generated. The same feeling of success can be generated in the business by working on problems and opportunities.

To ensure that your organisation takes ownership of the concept, here are a few ideas to help:

1. **Add your name** to the title (or make one up such as The Acme Idea Factory or The Acme "Too Good To Believe" Idea Factory Machine). Make it fun and perhaps a little silly. Create the expectation that this is meant to be relaxed and fun, yet focused to get results.

2. **Talk to the people** about the Idea Factory before any formal announcements are made. The most successful workshops and "ideas" strategies will be those which harness the experience and energy of the team in a single direction. You may have to sell the concept to one person at a time. That's fine because you want long-term results. Create a story around the need for more innovative thinking. People relate more to stories than corporate strategies. Stories focus on how, why and the morale or benefit; strategies focus on what.

3. **Involve a team of people.** Find out if there are any historical reasons why people would be suspicious of such a process. This needs to be sorted out before any launch. Then your first step is

to talk about the need for ideas within the organisation and how you believe that this system will work for the organisation and the people in it.

4. **Identify the skills** you have in your organisation already and those you need. Often, people have experience in previous jobs that you may not be aware of. Also, ask about the volunteer experience staff have. This may come from sitting on a sporting, social, cultural or church group board.

5. **Set up your first Idea Factory** to talk about the system to sell your team on the idea and to agree on how the system should work for your organisation. This is your first result and it is significant!

Taking ownership of the concept means using the philosophy of the Idea Factory pledge in your daily decision making. Staff and other managers will quickly recognise any hidden motives you may have. Learn from the mistakes that many organisations have made—take ownership of the program and generate enthusiasm for it, and do so with integrity.

2. Decide what you want to achieve

Before you can find the solution to any problem, you must be able to define the problem. The same applies to creating an opportunity. The biggest challenge for achieving either is producing a clear definition of what you want to achieve. That's your "Challenge".

A well-defined challenge is a short description of the main issues, in much the same way that a job description describes a job. It gives you the overall expectations and a general description. Often, once we have a clearly defined "challenge", the problem actually becomes quiet solvable for two key reasons:

1. It ensures that you understand and define the problem and its symptoms. The act of putting it in writing helps define the real issues.

2. It provides an incentive to think about the issues before the workshop to help everyone start with the same understanding.

The Challenge is very important to the overall process. Ensure that it is not too broad for one event. For example, it is highly unlikely that you can solve a number of different problems in one sitting. The Challenge is very important to the overall process. It can be very broad and general in nature. For example:

- The challenge is to consider new markets to expand our operation for 2003 and beyond.
- The challenge is to look at a range of new service opportunities as the market is starting to change.
- The challenge is to review our customer service approach because of the growing number of comments and complaints that we hear.
- The challenge is to review our sales force and our selling strategies to make them more effective.

The Challenge can also be quite specific. For example:

- The challenge is to fix a particular customer service problem for customer "Smith".
- The challenge is to improve our performance at this year's trade show.
- The challenge is to fix our employee compensation package to stop losing our best people.

Both types of challenge are suitable. However, be aware of the results that you will achieve from using each. The "general" challenge will tend to result in a series of strategies or ideas that will need further development. You may identify a new service that you believe to be worthwhile. In this case, you have taken an important first step but there are more steps to go. The other more specific challenge will generally result in a list of actions. Because your challenge is quite specific, you can reasonably be assured that you will talk about the key issues and conclude with a list of actions that must be taken to make your challenge work.

Start at the top

If you start with the first use of the Idea Factory, that is, to find the winning "idea" and then follow through to the action "to do" lists, you have already accomplished the hardest aspect of creating a new opportunity. You now have everything in place to make it work. By using the open concept of workshops, you have involved a number of people who each own a piece of the idea. This gives the idea momentum.

There is nothing more powerful in any organisation than momentum. You can use momentum the same way a coach uses it in sport. Watch any team that is doing well and you generally see energy on the players' faces. How often have you looked at a team that is losing and see that their body language makes them look like they have already lost the game? An organisation that is always reacting to the competition is exactly the same.

The Idea Factory process is one way to take the initiative and create some winning momentum for your organisation.

3. Set up a system to provide a quality result

Throughout the 1980s and 1990s, the quality movement introduced many useful tools and approaches to fix the numerous problems of business. One of the most useful tools, and perhaps the simplest one, involves applying two questions to your situation.

1. Are we doing the right thing?
2. Are we doing it the right way?

If you answer "yes" to question one (and your customers, staff and suppliers would also agree with you) then you are heading in the right direction. You can then find better ways to deliver the results. If you answer "no", it is time to start over. The Idea Factory is the right system for developing ideas. Now look at the best way to do it. At the very heart of the Idea Factory "production" system is a workshop. There are three phases for every workshop. Before beginning the workshop, use the following steps and guidelines to establish the system in your organisation:

Timing of the Idea Factory

Pick a regular time and day of the week or month to hold your workshops. Find time during the day when the energy levels of people are high. You want their best contribution. Resist the temptation to have people stay after work. They are contributing their ideas already. Is it fair to ask for their time as well?

Location for the Idea Factory

Pick a good location, one that eliminates distractions such as the telephone. It must be relaxing, comfortable and preferably informal. Distractions will kill your energy and enthusiasm.

Picking your Idea Factory team

Consider the team of people that you will use. Most often you will involve some co-workers in the process. You should also consider a wider range of people as well. Consider using one or two outsiders to contribute specific skills not found inside a company. Consider a variety of people within the company. You need people who will not always agree with the "boss". Often, staff who are not as familiar with your understanding of the issues (and your biases and opinions on the issues) may offer a useful perspective. Others to consider are:

- Customers who are good thinkers.
- Suppliers, retailers or others from your industry (who have something to gain from your success).
- Professionals such as accountants, consultants or public relations people who have experience across different sectors.
- A local university business professor.
- Directors or managers from other companies.

Consider a specialist such as a market researcher. They can add a unique dimension by telling you how society is changing. The implications may be valuable. If a project is to be useful and successful, it must reflect these changes. In addition, consider the skills people have gained from their previous employers and their outside interests. There are many people who have manual jobs yet are involved at an executive level in various charity, hobby and not-for-profit organisations.

Look for people who are good at problem-solving and developing systems for their work. These skills are very necessary for effective brainstorming. You need people who can see both the "trees" and the "forest". These are the people who listen to the comments from one customer and see how the same issue impacts on many others. They are the kind of people who are frustrated if they can't resolve a problem and insist on working on it until they get a result.

A word of warning when selecting people—at times you may encounter people who think of themselves as highly creative already. Depending on the individual, keep an eye on their openness to new thinking and the use of various creativity techniques. They often feel it unnecessary to participate actively and prefer to "jump to a solution". This is not likely to result in a new or unique solution. It also hinders consensus that could result from the group activity.

The success of the workshop event will be related to two factors:

1. The importance that management places on innovative thinking and the Idea Factory.
2. The staff's perception of the importance that management places on innovative thinking and the Idea Factory.

If the people at the top of the business believe that the continual flow of new ideas is critical to the success of the organisation, then the "team" will respond. If not, their contribution will be less than 100 per cent effective. Therefore do not schedule other meetings during this period. Tell everyone else to clear their meetings. The test will come when someone has an urgent customer meeting and wants to skip the Idea Factory. What should they do?

On one hand, the customer has a right to attention. On the other hand, the meeting could be solving problems that will help 100 customers. Be prepared for this situation. What will you do? What will you recommend for the team to do? How does your decision to participate or not participate influence the success of the program? Prepare for these situations and look at the impact of your decisions. They will send a signal to everyone. Recognise these signals before you send out the wrong ones.

Preparation for your first innovation session

Before the first session, ensure people understand the need for greater innovative thinking and the Idea Factory processes. This book and any materials you want to prepare would be very useful.

In fact, the first session is probably best spent teaching the system. One of the first principles to teach is preparation. This includes understanding the challenge, and time spent to consider the issue from various perspectives, and some tentative issues, ideas or questions. This will create an expectation and a focus on results. The system outlined in this book is similar to a software program. Once you buy the program you also must learn how to use it. Anyone who has tried new software will also know that you need to practise until you can use the software to its fullest potential. The Idea Factory is the same. Practise and it will improve. Other points to consider:

1. Once you define the Idea Factory Challenge, distribute a copy to everyone several days in advance of the workshop. This shows organisation and professionalism of the intent.
2. Ask everyone to consider the Challenge from their perspective and to make notes if appropriate. Participants may also want to bring in some research, examples or other aids that will add something to the overall effort.
3. Arrange for some refreshment...water, coffee, sandwiches or whatever your team will prefer. Consider using some music because it can add to the mood of any event by relaxing people or energising them. Stay away from alcohol, as it does not encourage creativity in the least.

Your Idea Factory workshop

There are many ways to run a workshop. The following steps are given to help you start the process. You are best to use these to start but consider how you can make it fit your organisation better. As with any process, make it work for you by adapting whatever changes are necessary. Remember that this is your system. You own it. Its success depends upon the team.

Phase 1: the warm-up

This phase should take around 30 minutes of a two-hour session.

1. Open the event with a review of the Challenge.

2. Present the background issues to the Challenge. This may include a fuller description of the need or reason for the Challenge, any comments or research that were used to create it, and so on. Give everyone a few minutes to think about it.

3. Have each participant comment on the issue from their perspective. Give everyone the opportunity to lay their cards on the table. What is their position? Their bias? Their stake in the issue? By giving people the Challenge prior to the workshop, they will have had time to prepare their initial thoughts.

4. This last step is important—get everyone talking and participating. If someone seems to be very quiet, find out why and get him or her involved.

Phase 2: the brainstorming

There are two basic ways to brainstorm:

One way is to freewheel by keeping everything completely unstructured and getting everyone to simply suggest the first thing that comes to mind. As long as everyone is participating on an equal footing, this approach can work well. Get as many options or ideas involving your Challenge as possible. This is not the time to judge ideas. It is simply the time to create a list as long as you can.

It is critical to build in a sense of excitement and enthusiasm among the participants. Freewheeling needs to be facilitated by someone who people can motivate and bring in line if they start to dominate the session. Once you believe that you have a good list of options or ideas, start at the top of the list and discuss each to highlight any obviously great ideas and eliminate any bad ones.

Eventually one or two ideas rise to the top of the pile. To test the strength of these ideas, go back to the original challenge and ask the group, "Does this idea really satisfy the challenge?"

Even if it does, consider how you could add to the idea to make it stronger or more beneficial to the customer. Always strive to maximise the benefits to the customer (as long as the benefit provides more value than it will cost the customer). Remember that it is better to aim high and settle for slightly less then to aim low and reach it.

Test your idea—could your competitor come up with the same solution?

If so, you should go back to find a better idea.

In the long term there is no point in simply keeping up with your competitors. Change the rules of the game before they do!

Using the Idea Factory tools

Another way to find ideas is to use any of the Idea Factory tools as a starting point for your workshop (a variety of tools are provided in Section Two). Each has been designed to provide a series of perspectives and questions that you can use to lead the discussions.

These tools reflect a wide variety of strategies that you can use very quickly. The key points for using any tool include:

- Select the tools most appropriate for your situation and the task at hand.
- Read through it and recognise how the various questions and issues may be useful for starting the workshop.
- Copy the appropriate papers for each member of the team in order that they can read it before the start of your workshop.
- Each tool is designed to inform and educate. Once you use a "tool" the questions and concepts involved with each can be used over and over again.
- Each tool is a pathway to a destination. If you have a better way to get your ideas, use it!

Phase 3: the results

Each workshop must conclude with a result. This may be a list of good ideas, a well-developed concept that you will work on or a list of actions to complete a project. These should be considered the tangible results of the workshop. The second type of result is the benefits of finding a group solution to a problem. There is tremendous value to any organisation that builds a spirit of "co-operative competition" within it to work on such ideas. The co-operative aspect brings together different people who have different backgrounds and experience. Each will see the situation in their own way. The competitive element acts as a balance to ensure that the ideas are good enough.

> **Test your idea—*could your competitor come up with the same solution?***
>
> **If so, you should go back to find a better idea.**
>
> **In the long term there is no point in simply keeping up with your competitors. Change the rules of the game before they do!**

Someone needs to pull people together and yet people must be able to think in their own unique way to continually review the options to enhance ideas. Co-operative competition is the pursuit of the best ideas by harnessing the full experience and intuition of people. At times, this may lead to some conflicts. As long as people maintain their focus on the Challenge, they will avoid any perceived personal criticisms.

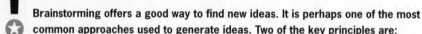

THE BASICS OF BRAINSTORMING

Brainstorming offers a good way to find new ideas. It is perhaps one of the most common approaches used to generate ideas. Two of the key principles are:

1. Quantity of ideas is more important than quality (at first).
2. Defer judgement on any idea until all ideas are raised.

Brainstorming is something you can do by yourself or in groups. Here are some tips for brainstorming with groups to find ideas in your business. The key steps are:

1. Define the PROBLEM OR OPPORTUNITY in the form of a question, using terms everyone can understand.

2. Choose your PARTICIPANTS, usually three to six people. Try to involve a decision-maker or budget-holder to allow them to experience the whole process, from the raw initial idea to a solution. Select people who can offer a range of perspectives. Perhaps use an outsider, too.

3. Set your TIME AND PLACE. Make sure people can attend. Choose a good environment that is creative in some way. Review the section of establishing your Idea Factory in this book.

4. Select someone to lead who can FACILITATE. At times they have to control any negative attitudes, enhance existing ideas, encourage people to speak up or add new ideas. A hard job at times but very important.

Sometimes the ideal solution is found and everyone sees it. If not, narrow down ideas into two or three categories or groupings. Usually common themes can be found. Get people to combine ideas into stronger ones. If you need a decision on one idea, have people vote. The highest one or two advance and become your focus. You may want to combine the top ideas into something bigger.

Lastly, you do not need a group to brainstorm. Many people are very effective in brainstorming by themselves but they still use the same basic process and discipline to spark their imagination and shape new ideas.

Creating your Idea Factory Challenge

Every time you have a brainstorming workshop, take a few minutes to define the challenge.

 This sets the agenda for the session and allows a continual focus on achieving the results. Create a model page like the following that captures the key points on a single page. In this case, your goal is a better trade show presentation. The benefit? A stronger image within your industry and more sales! The Idea Factory workshop results you should expect are a series of ideas that will enhance your trade show presentation and success.

IDEA FACTORY CHALLENGE

The Challenge
The industry tradeshow is coming up in May. Our present booth does not get us noticed as the professional and innovative company we are. Our challenge is to improve our presentation at the show to generate new leads and build stronger relationships with existing customers and people who refer business to us.

Background points
- *Our budget is only $2500, how can we maximise this?*
- *How can we get our suppliers involved in joint projects?*
- *What materials should we develop? Do we need to train people who "sell" at our booth?*
- *With 200 other suppliers, how can we stand out?*

Points I want to raise, discuss, research:

Results from today's workshop

Details: Friday morning, 10:00 to 11:30, meeting room, EB, SS, TM, NP and SG

The Challenge
Describe the problem or opportunity in a couple of sentences—what, why, how, etc.

Add some key points.

This section is for participants to make their own notes prior to the workshop.

Include a section to record results—from the participant's perspective.

Include the details: time, location, length, team participants, etc.

Insights
from Chapter Four

- ✪ Finding ideas and opportunities is not a simple and rational process. You cannot dictate that people must be "creative" as if you can turn on some switch.
- ✪ Plan now to move as quickly as possible through three strategies for innovation:
  1. Take ownership of the need to challenge the business to be more innovative and be prepared to walk the talk.
  2. Define what you want to achieve.
  3. Set up a system and process.
- ✪ The quality of results is important. Test your idea—could your competitor come up with the same solution? If so, find a better idea. In the long term there is no point in simply keeping up with your competitors. Change the rules of the game before they do.

Convert these insights into **action** for your organisation.

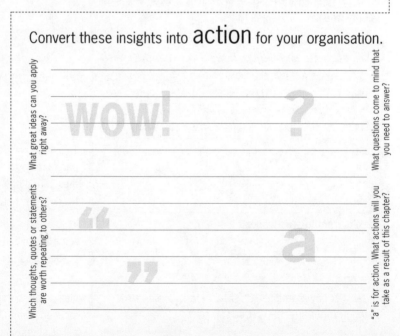

What great ideas can you apply right away?

Which thoughts, quotes or statements are worth repeating to others?

What questions come to mind that you need to answer?

"a" is for action. What actions will you take as a result of this chapter?

the
innovative
thinkers' tool kit
to achieve
results

part two

5 the idea factory tool kit

There are many creativity tools that you can use during workshops and meetings to provoke new ways of thinking about business challenges. They are designed to ask questions or to provide a new perspective that you apply to your situation.

The series of tools in this section were used during numerous workshops. Many were challenges that were developed to achieve a specific result for an organisation but clearly have value to a wider audience. They will not give you the answers but they will provide you with different perspectives that prompt people to think in different ways to find new types of solutions. Use them as the agenda for your workshops. They will direct the questions and the outcomes.

Your objective is to use these tools like a carpenter uses his or her tool kit. You pick the right tool for the job. You are certainly not restricted to these tools. Many of the books on creativity and brainstorming have lots of ideas to help you look outside the traditional ways of doing things; this is particularly true for problem-solving. The amount of information available to provide assistance and ideas for problem-solving is enormous. Combine your experience with these tools to find the necessary solutions to your problems.

From the "opportunities" perspective, the questions and challenges raised are designed to look at different aspects of the organisation and decide what kinds of opportunities you want to create.

One way to think about the differences between these two is to think of problems in this way. Your customers do not like the way you deliver your goods to their office and they want you to do it their way. The problem is clear. You know how you do it today and your customer tells you how they want the goods delivered. Your job is to ensure that you follow their directions.

However, sometimes the problem is more complex. Instead of a customer telling which way to go, they say they want to you to do "better". You scratch your head and wonder what "better" means. Is this faster? Cheaper? More accurate? More friendly? Or whatever? You ask them and they say that they really don't know.

Your challenge is now to come up with a number of options to see what the customer feels will be useful. This is a much greater challenge, as there is not a single right answer but a series of possible answers.

How to use these tools

Read each tool to see how it can be useful to you. Each was written for a specific purpose. Read over the issues and questions that it asks. Does it fit with your challenges within the business? Each provides some background points that you and your team should read and learn from. It won't make you an expert but it will get you started on the right path. It will also be useful to talk to each team member before your workshop about the specific issues associated with each tool. In all cases, modify them to fit your situation.

Copy these pages and give them to those participating in the workshop. They will provide everyone with a basic overview of the issues involved.

Tools for your Idea Factory

Consider the "tools" of the Idea Factory to be your agenda, as in a meeting agenda. The agenda guides the discussion and helps to shape the final result. The same applies to the tools of creativity. There is a range of categories of tools that you can consider.

1. To find new ideas

There are a wide variety of excellent books that offer many creativity techniques for finding new ideas through structured technique.

Tool 1—An example of idea boxes is used as an example of
these techniques

Books that are full of techniques often seem trivial. However, these are the techniques that businesses have used to find new insights that lead to new product and service concepts. Consider these books for your tool kit:

- *Applied Imagination*, written by Alex Osborn in 1953, makes for a fascinating read as he is credited with creating the term "brainstorming". His ideas are still very relevant today. It may be hard to find as it is out of print.
- *Thinkertoys, A Handbook of Business Creativity for the '90s* by Michael Michalko (Ten Speed Books, Berkeley, California).
- *Five Star Mind* by Tom Wujec is full of games and puzzles to stimulate your creativity and imagination (Doubleday Book, Toronto).
- *Aha! 10 Ways to Free Your Creative Spirit and Find Your Great Ideas* by Jordon Ayan (Crown Trade Paperbacks, New York).
- *Deliberate Cre8ive Thinking* by Bill Jarrard and Jennifer Goddard at www.mindwerx.com.au
- *Ideas Generation* by Tim Flattery and Rosemary Herceg provides a 21-step process for generating ideas. www.ideasgeneration.com.au
- Books by Edward de Bono, including *Six Thinking Hats, Parallel Thinking* and *Serious Creativity* offer many interesting perspectives. Also see www.debono.org

2. To help find ideas that lead to new ways of competing

The tools listed below are specific in the sense that each is designed to focus on a particular aspect of a business. Use them to explore the sources of new ideas to improve or expand your opportunities.

Tool 2—Efficiency and effectiveness check-up!
Tool 3—Re-invent your organisation
Tool 4—The millennium challenge
Tool 5—Make your customers money! Save your customers money!
Tool 6—The "4Ps" versus "3Es"
Tool 7—Focus on customers or clients
Tool 8—Audit your stakeholders
Tool 9—The profit tool: profits = revenues − expenses

3. To enhance your ideas

Useful references include Edward de Bono's thinking tool, "Six Thinking Hats".

Tool 10—Idea Factory insights into action framework

4. To help plan the execution of your ideas

Having a great idea is one thing—acting on it is another. Every great idea needs a plan to make it happen. The great idea provides the vision and direction of where you want to go and to find strategies to guide the way, while action plans provide the "check lists" of specific actions necessary to get the results.

Tool 11—Develop better strategy
Tool 12—Create winning action plans
Tool 13—Create your own knowledge tools

The idea box

tool
1

Idea Boxes combine elements of an idea into new and bigger ideas. These elements are the characteristics, factors or variables of the challenge you are dealing with. For this exercise, pick a challenge that is open to many options. This is particularly good in a marketing context when you are trying to create new concepts. Study the example below to understand this approach. It is very powerful for finding totally new ideas. Here are your instructions:

1. Write down your challenge.
2. Select the parameters of your challenge and list them across the box.
3. List options for each parameter. List as many as you wish. You can brainstorm with others to generate this list.
4. When the box is filled with options, make random runs through the lists linking one or more from each column and then combining them into entirely new forms.
5. Write down the new ideas and concepts along the right-hand side of the box.

For example, let's talk about laundry hampers. The parameters are the materials we can use, the shapes of hampers, the finishes we can use, and the location of the hamper. For the idea search, at random pick variations and connect them to create a new concept. These random connections may trigger new ideas and concepts.

Your Challenge...

create a new design for a laundry hamper

Parameters ⇒ Options ⇓	Material	Shape	Finish	Location	New Concepts
1.	Wicker	Square	Natural	Sits on Floor	1.
2.	Plastic	**Cylinder****	**Painted****	On Ceiling	2.
3.	Paper	Rectangle	Clear	**On Wall****	3.
4.	Metal	Hexagonal	Luminous	To Basement	4.
5.	**Netting****	Cube	Neon	On Door	5.

**Make this connection. In a workshop, the group combined Netting, Cylinder, Painted and On Wall. It created a successful new laundry hamper concept. See Thinkertoys for a fuller explanation of this Idea Box and actual product that was created.

Your idea box challenge

Here are your instructions:

- Write down your challenge.

- Select the parameters of your challenge and list them across the box.

- List options for each parameter. List as many as you wish. You can brainstorm with others to generate this list.

- When the box is filled with options, make random runs through the lists linking one or more from each column and then combining them into entirely new forms.

- Write down the new ideas and concepts along the right-hand side of the box.

Your Challenge...

Parameters ⇒ Options ⇓		New Concepts
1.		1.
2.		2.
3.		3.
4.		4.
5.		5.

Efficiency and effectiveness check-up!

To be efficient without being effective achieves little. Yet to be effective without being efficient is a luxury that few can afford in today's marketplace. The inefficient use of resources is regarded as bad management. Use an Idea Factory to review your organisation or in services or systems. Can you become (1) more efficient in the delivery of your services or products, (2) more effective in their delivery, or (3) or can you improve both? Consider the definitions for your organisation:

tool 2

1. A working definition of efficiency—are we doing things the right way?

2. A working definition of effectiveness—are we doing the right things?

You can be highly effective in your job or as a company and yet be highly inefficient. The difference is important to understand. Though we aim for both, it is better to be effective and inefficient than the reverse. Why? Being highly efficient in providing mediocre services does not help you achieve business goals.

Although we tend to assume that efficiency means doing things more "cheaply", it has a broader meaning when you consider "total quality" issues. Once we know the systems are basically effective, we can then make them more efficient (using less resources to do the same thing). Often, too much focus is placed on efficiency. We need to expand our skills to include "effectiveness" in our tool box of management skills.

Accomplishing efficiency is often easier than reaching effectiveness. The reason is quite simple. To undertake an activity more efficiently, we generally look at the actions to see if some components can be made cheaper, faster or produced in a different way. We already know the outcome we are searching for but we need a better way to reach it. However, effectiveness can be much more complicated.

Now consider the specific points:

- Effectiveness: Are you doing the right things? Asking the right questions? Tackling the right problems? How can you increase the value to customers? If you spent $1.00 to get a certain result last year, how can you get $1.10 of benefit by spending $1.00 this year? How can you create more value?

- Efficiency: Are we doing things right? Are we taking unnecessary steps? If you spent $1.00 last year to get a certain result how can you reduce this to 90 cents to accomplish the same result this year?

Your long-term goal is to combine both efficiency and effectiveness to get $1.10 value for 90 cents.

Your workshop challenge

When thinking about a specific service, approach, process or company activities, consider these questions...

- Why are we undertaking this activity?
- Whose benefit is it for? Is the benefit greater than the cost?
- Are the perceived benefits actually going to benefit the customer?
- How can the customers benefit even more?
- Do we need to do it at all?
- Can we define the elements that we can improve?

From this discussion, conclude by adding the best ideas to your plans.

Re-invent your organisation

If you had to re-design your organisation, how would it look? Would your services be different? Would you have a different corporate structure? Would your selection criteria for staff, suppliers or customers be different? The answers to these and related questions can offer valuable insights for re-developing your organisation.

Here is a situation that often happens in business. The dominant company in the industry grows larger and larger. Along the way it starts to alienate some workers who decide to set up their own business in competition with the original company. They have spent months and maybe even years thinking about the ways that they could do it better. The irony is that often the most innovative people are those who leave the organisation after taking full advantage of the training and personal development they were entitled to.

tool

3

Your workshop challenge

An Idea Factory could be an ideal way to focus on the changes that you could make if you started over. Consider:

- What constraints do you have that someone starting the business today would not have?

- Would the rules of the industry be different in some way?

- How would you take advantage of the long established companies if you wanted to enter a new market?

- What are the weak spots in the industry?

- How would you go about getting the best people, technology and systems, and so on in the industry?

With this information as a base, start to re-design your services or production process as if you could start over. Use a flow chart approach to identify each key step along the way.

Work through your re-design without being held back by your existing business realities.

Conclude your Idea Factory session by challenging the team to satisfy these concerns:

1. Of all of the ideas and observations that were created during the workshop, which has the potential to damage your existing business the most?

2. Conversely, if you could make one or more changes, which have the greatest potential to add to your success?

3. Decide which is most important to your business to work on—the threats or the opportunities?

4. What prevents you from implementing these changes? Define the specific issues that would prevent you from advancing the problem.

5. Could you actually find a way to create a breakthrough to gain the benefit of the changes?

6. What actions can you take, both short term and long term, that would improve your organisation?

This approach for re-inventing your organisation can be used in a general way or very specific way to focus on particular systems or services. It is very powerful. The objective is to appreciate how someone else can move into your market and take over your customers or services without being restricted by history, tradition or myth.

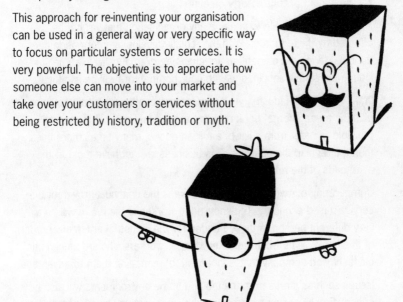

The millennium challenge: challenging your past to create your future

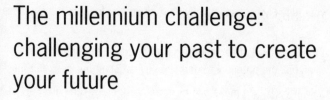

The Millennium Challenge creates an opportunity to reflect on the many changes that have occurred during the past 100 years and, in fact, the past 1,000 years. The impact of the following three factors will be critical to all organisations as we head into the new Millennium:

tool
4

- The impact of **change** on the industry, staff, customers and suppliers.

- The impact of **competition** on your business and the industry, and where competition may come from.

- The impact of **technology** on everything.

It is almost impossible to imagine any organisation that will not be affected by these factors. With the rapidly developing information age, the boundaries of competition are changing dramatically. In some industries, simply anticipating who your competitors will be is difficult.

In the retail book industry, your competitors can be the local bookshop plus the mega Internet book retailers around the world. It is already possible to order from a list of a million books, many times more titles than the regular shop carries. This business will not have most of the overheads of the retail industry.

Complicating our workplace of the future is the continual growth of the service-based economy. The knowledge worker of the future will be a very different person to those needed for the industrial era. Many readers of this book will be frustrated "knowledge" workers who are stuck in an old-fashioned company that is incapable of managing them to advantage.

Issues such as stress from the job and home environments will also be critical. Employees who are stressed cannot produce innovation as easily as those who are relaxed and enjoying what they do.

Your workshop challenge

Challenge your business to consider the impact of these factors. This session can only conclude with a result to "continue" to focus on these factors, but that is a good result. Along the way, you will find a dozen small ideas that you can take advantage of now—before your competitors do. Some issues for each factor include:

1. The impact of change—staff, customers (and future customers) and suppliers will all need to consider the impact of change. This reflects changes to the business and to the people involved in the business. You must consider change in terms of services, markets, customers and the human aspect of this change. What is the impact on workers in terms of stress and wellness, education needs and so on?

2. The impact of competition—one of the major challenges for all organisations is to define which direction competition will come from. The rules are continually changing. Is the biggest threat a competitor or complacency? With good strategies and continual innovation, your business can survive and continue to grow.

3. The impact of technology—the impact of technology on business is another major dilemma. You must live with it, use it and love it. If not, you are obsolete. Technology will bring overseas markets and competitors closer all the time. How much potential does the Internet have for your business? What are the threats? What are the opportunities?

Each of these three factors encompasses a range of issues for your business

1. Organise small group sessions to look at each issue and summarise its importance to the business.

2. Conclude with two or three recommendations, considerations or issues to develop.

3. Review the results of the session and consider what additional "raw materials" would have helped?

Make your customers money! Save your customers money!

Someone once said that the only way to make money in business is to show your customers how to make money or how to save money. Not bad advice. Any organisation which sells to other businesses has only one purpose, and that is to help its customers either make money or save money by using its services and products.

Your workshop challenge

Start with a list of your products or services and start to answer two questions:

1. How can you help your customers save more money?

2. How can you help your customers make money?

For example, are your customers potential customers for each other? You can organise networking breakfasts that introduce customers to customers and help make this business happen. Accountants and lawyers do this regularly. Your customer will remember where these contacts came from.

Also, can you organise workshops or seminars or any other kinds of information service to help your customers to better use your services or products? There is a tremendous benefit to helping customers to better use your services.

Use this workshop to list five ways to create some opportunities for your customers to learn, gain and share or whatever it takes to make and save money. They will love you for it. Your image will improve and you will be better able to retain your customers and by building strong relationships they may actually buy more from you.

The "4Ps" versus "3Es"

Review your marketing priorities. Many of the traditional marketing textbooks talk about the "4Ps" of marketing; place, product, promotion and price. This framework is often used as the model for many of our marketing plans. However, how useful is this approach to a service organisation?

Use the Idea Factory to define the issues most important to people such as the impact of the service you provide, the delivery of your services and the way you provide "total quality" in your work.

Keep your focus on "service" rather than taking a "product" orientation. Although many would argue that there is little difference from a marketing perspective, the research into marketing systems is now revealing that there are benefits to be gained from looking at services in new ways.

tool
6

Consider how the approaches would differ if you decided that your marketing activities must achieve the 3Es for your members (and potential members):

Traditional view of marketing	The buyer's perspective
Price	Entice—How can you entice potential customers to your business or organisation?
Product	Enthuse—How can you enthuse prospective customers to use your services or products?
Place	Excite—How can you excite them to continue to buy your products or services?
Promotion	

The traditional view looks at the tools we can use rather than at the outcomes we are looking for. Service marketing must also consider how the services are packaged and how they are delivered to create "value". All organisations must create value for their customers. Ask your people how your business entices customers, enthuses them to buy and excites customers to stay (and to refer new business to your organisation).

Your workshop challenge

In your workshop find three to five ways to entice, enthuse and excite.

1. Entice new customers—How can you entice potential customers to your business or organisation?

2. Enthuse new customers—How can you enthuse prospective customers to use your services or products?

3. Excite new customers—How can you excite them to continue to buy your products or services?

The final aspect is creating your action plan and budget to make it happen!

Focus on customers or clients

Most service businesses will earn most of next year's revenues from today's customers. To protect these customers, create a customer service management system to ensure your customers are satisfied with your services and the delivery of these services.

You can create a Customer Service Action Plan to reach three key goals:

1. Keep the existing customers.

2. Encourage the use of additional services or products.

3. Develop stronger relationships with customers.

First, define the overall focus or theme for your customer service efforts for the year. For example:

Secure our existing services and market our services to provide (1) related design services and (2) services to a wider group of branch offices.

tool
7

Below is a framework based on three key goals that you can use to create a customer service system. These are only guidelines and should be tailored to your style and approach.

1. Actions to keep the existing customers

What is the customer's perception of your quality and service? Focus on finding ways to improve the services provided, to encourage communication, and to deliver services in ways that better respond to the needs of customers.

2. Actions to encourage the use of additional services or products

What else can you sell to existing customers? Help the existing customers identify other service needs that help them to accomplish their business goals.

3. Actions to develop stronger relationships with clients

Improve, strengthen and develop your business and social relationships with the key decision-makers (both today's and tomorrow's) of each customer.

Generally, a one-page plan with five to 10 actions is all that is necessary for each major customer. Some professional service firms use this type of system for their top 50 clients.

You will recognise that the actions will be similar for each customer. This gives you opportunities to develop systems to become both efficient and effective with your customer service planning. Do include specifics—what are we going to do? when are you going to do it? how much it will cost (time and dollars)?

Your workshop challenge

If you target your top five customers with a customer management plan, you will build a stronger relationship with your customers.

1. Discuss the framework above and adapt it for your organisation.

2. List your five key customers or clients.

3. Brainstorm on the actions that will achieve these objectives over the next twelve months for each client or customer.

4. Create the action plan to make it happen.

5. Review these customer service management plans to keep track of the progress of the actions defined in the plans.

Audit your stakeholders

Use an Idea Factory to develop a stronger understanding of those who are important to the success of your business. Customers are only one group that a business must consider.

What is a stakeholder?

A stakeholder is anyone or group with an interest in your organisation. This is best measured by someone who can influence your organisation or be influenced by it.

Who are your stakeholders?

- Identify your stakeholders among those individuals internal to your organisation and those external to it.

- Internal stakeholders specific to your business—members, staff, employees, volunteers (also by division or other classification), or others who benefit from your work.

- External stakeholders specific to your business—suppliers, competitors, customers.

- External stakeholders—government agencies, educational institutes, other not-for-profit organisations, media, politicians.

What is at "stake"?

The first step is recognising who your stakeholders are.

The second step is understanding what "stake" each group has. This is particularly important and often under-developed. Perhaps a better way to look at this issue is to consider what is the "selfish interest" of each stakeholder group? This represents a much stronger perspective than the typical marketing jargon of understanding the needs of stakeholders. The "selfish interest" would encompass needs, wants and desires. By understanding the "selfish interests" of stakeholders, create "win win" opportunities for each stakeholder.

The third step is to rank the relative importance of each stakeholder. This is a crucial step as all stakeholders are not of equal value to your organisation's success.

Your workshop challenge

The key steps in stakeholder management are:

1. Identify the key stakeholders in the organisation.

2. Determine the roles each stakeholder plays in (or for) the organisation.

3. Determine how each stakeholder group measures its performance (eg its selfish interest).

4. Generate objectives from each stakeholder group as an aid to organisational planning.

5. Begin the process of satisfying both the stakeholder and organisation's needs.

By reviewing the key stakeholders of your organisation you create a framework for improving the image of your organisation and its ability to communicate with these important groups or individuals.

The profit tool:
profits = revenues – expenses

This tool is an exercise to study the relationship between profits, revenues and expenses. But this is not an accounting exercise. As a workshop exercise we must expand these terms to a wider series of concerns for business people.

- **Revenues**—How we view revenues must also include some discussion of the type of customers we want to service, the amount of challenge or learning that we want, and other benefits that add value to our lives and businesses. This is particularly important for family-owned or privately-owned businesses. You can also view revenues in terms of resources that you acquire that allow other important to happen.

- **Expenses**—Expenses not only include financial costs, they also include time, stress and our other limited resources. There are a tremendous number of stories about executives who walked away from successful careers because they had not balanced their needs for healthy emotional, spiritual, financial and career goals.

- **Profits**—Traditionally, the meaning given to profit, or the return on investment, simply reflects money. For many of today's professionals, home office workers, and owners of small and medium sized businesses, the rate of return is not strictly a financial calculation. It also reflects security, lifestyle, peace of mind and so on. How does your business define the term profit? What is important to the long-term viability of your business?

Your workshop challenge
The purpose of the workshop is to maximise our "profit" in whatever terms you define it by:

1. Defining two or three strategies that you will follow to increase the revenues in the numerator.

2. Defining two or three strategies that you will do to decrease the expenses in the denominator.

Note that you will be going against the trend in many of today's organisations. It seems that we have virtually put all our time into finding efficiencies (reducing the expenses). Most business publications tell you about techniques to cut back, save more, etc. That's fine, but recognise the simple truth that you can also increase your return by increasing revenues.

Use your workshop to define a year-long action plan to increase your revenues and decrease your expenses. Because you can't do everything at once, make this a year-long project but plan today to start each activity with a similar workshop to expand the project. The long-term benefit can be tremendous as you can focus on problems rather than jumping between them.

Idea Factory insights into action framework

The director of a large transport business once said that her company didn't need new ideas. "We have lots of ideas," she said, "we just don't have the time to do anything with them."

What she didn't say was that ideas are hard work, and they need time and energy. That's why we often shy away from new ideas and fail to find the time to make them happen. This company badly needed to grow its profits. It was clear that they saw the creative process as a two-step process of finding an idea and then implementing it. They find an idea and then define the actions to make it happen. The company failed to discover that by adding a couple of steps, it could achieve two important challenges for innovation:

tool
10

- Nurturing the imagination and intuition of the employees to create value for the business.

- This is important to maximise the potential of the ideas that are chosen.

Instead of this two-step process, try a different model that is comprised of four steps:

1. use your **insights** to find great…

2. **ideas** but create the…

3. **opportunity** before defining the…

4. **actions** to implement the great ideas.

By adding these steps you form a more viable vision of the successful idea in action. You start the momentum that's critical to making a great idea succeed. Invest your time in creating the opportunity before you decide to pursue an idea. By doing so you fuel the momentum you need that makes great opportunities hard to ignore. It's easy to sit on a good idea. Everyone does that from time to time. But momentum makes it hard to sit on a great opportunity. You can't ignore it because the potential is too obvious.

Your insights lead to ideas, which you shape into opportunities and then action plans. Use this framework to build successful business ideas.

1. Nurture your insights

Insights come from harnessing your intuition and taking the time to observe and understand.

- What have you become aware of or noticed?
- What intrigues you?
- What has come to your attention?

Insights lead to great ideas throughout all stages of innovation.

2. The great idea

In a couple of sentences describe your idea as if you had to explain it to someone else. Get your idea clearly formulated.

- What is the idea? How does it work? What does it involve?
- Who will benefit? What purpose does it serve? What does it make possible?
- What is great about your idea? Why is it exciting? What is better or different about it?

3. Create the opportunity

Create the opportunity by expanding your great idea to its fullest potential. Add a page or two of related detail to describe the successful idea in action. Think as if anything is possible. What would you love to do?

- Find three options or features to enhance the value of your idea. Can you find any more?
- Think in terms of enhancing the idea in the short, medium and long term. What options do you have to enhance the idea at each phase?
- How can you create synergy through partnerships, joint promotions or alternative ways of implementing the idea?
- What is the bigger context? How can it create value and growth? What are the key revenue sources, both today and for the long term?

4. Define the actions!

List critical actions required to make the opportunity a reality. Your planning must be thorough yet realistic. Successful action plans build efficiency and effectiveness into every element of the plan.

- What would have to be in place for it to work?
- What are the first three things you need to do to get started?
- What is the biggest weakness you must overcome? What will you do to prevent failure?

the insight

the idea

the opportunity

the actions

Develop innovative strategies

Every business sets goals for what it wants to achieve. However, many fail to reach these goals. This often relates to the lack of proper understanding of "strategy". Many strategic plans have little to do with strategy; they resemble basic to-do lists. They list actions that may or may not achieve the goals. It's often hard to tell. Rule number one for developing good strategies is to understand the difference between what you want to achieve and how you want to achieve it. Consider:

- A goal is what you want to achieve.

- A strategy is how you want to achieve the goal.

Once you have defined these, you need to set your tactics—*the specific actions needed for each strategy to achieve the goal.* You create a "to do" list to achieve its strategy, not the goal.

Note if you skip the strategy stage, you may bypass opportunities, as you will not ask, "Is this the best way to reach our goal?" Unless strategies are developed properly, you cannot be sure that they are the most effective approaches. In other words, you may be happy making $1.00 by using a specific tactic. However, by expanding your options, the opportunity could be worth $2.00.

Here's a useful way to understand this process. Imagine that your goal is to project a modern image of your business. Because customers often visit your premises, one of your strategies may be to renovate your offices to project a consistent modern image. Your tactics will include a long list of actions such as painting, providing new carpets and so on. From a business perspective, you could cost the entire renovation strategy and then compare it to other strategies which may project a modern image such as advertising, public relations and introducing new services.

In reality, what often happens is that a dispute breaks out between those arguing over the colour of a new carpet and those wanting a new theme in the advertising. As you will appreciate, when the discussion is reduced to disputes of "tactics" very little will be accomplished. Stick to overall strategies and leave the tactics alone for a while!

Case study: increase sales

Here is another example. Your goal may be to increase sales by 10 per cent next year. How are you going to do this? One strategy may be to expand the sales force. Tactics may include:

- Define the "right" salesperson for the company.
- Advertise or recruit.
- Hire and train the person.

However, if you take another perspective, your strategy may be to implement a customer service review (to sort out problems and to talk to customers about their needs for the year). Your tactics may include:

- Identify the top 25 customers most important to the business.
- Develop a customer service "interview" that lists the key questions you need to ask.
- Call or meet one customer each day to get this information.
- Collate information and make it available to others for further thinking.
- Make any necessary changes that customer suggested.

Your discussion should involve the issues most important to your business. There is an expression that fits very well in this situation; *with which strategy do you get the "maximum bang for the buck"*? This is not a short-term perspective. Consider the long term. The best strategies follow the golden rule of working smarter, not harder.

Your workshop challenge

Set a challenge to develop one or more strategies for a given goal. How?

Pick a goal important to the business.

Make sure your team can separate strategies from tactics.

Define the business goal that you want to brainstorm.

Write an Idea Factory Challenge Page and distribute it to your team.

Questions to discuss:

- What have you done in the past? How well has it worked?
- How well could it work? How can you improve it?
- What do your customers say? Ask. Involve them.

- What is the traditional approach for your industry? What would break all the rules? How would another industry look at the goal?

Key steps to focus on:

1. Write down the proposed strategies. Discuss them (one at a time) to maximise the opportunity that each offers.

2. Consider their cost in terms of dollars, time and other resources for each.

3. Decide which is the best short-term solution and the best long-term solution? Which is the best solution for your business?

4. Consider the "opportunity" cost of not doing the strategy—what are you risking?

5. Which gives you the *maximum bang for the buck*?

Your strategy should be written in a way that is clear and easy to understand by those who will be use it.

Create winning action plans

Linked to each strategy (Tool 11) are specific action-oriented tasks that must be achieved to reach your objectives. Once you have identified your goals and strategies, define the specific actions that will get the results you need. This can be very straightforward. Get your team to produce a list of actions that are necessary to make something work (your to-do list). Tool 12 expands this to consider two simple concepts:

1. What must you do to get a result, to achieve your goals?

2. What must you avoid doing (or not doing) to prevent failing?

The first list is quite simple. The second is much harder.

Step one: the "success" to-do list

Start the workshop by writing the goal you want to achieve and the strategy you are using to do so. Consider:

* What you have to do to get the result.

* When it has to happen by—your deadlines.

* How you want to make it work.

* Who will undertake the work and be responsible for it.

* How much is it going to cost.

Use the team to develop ideas for making everything work. You can use a couple of approaches for this. Identify the people who will be on the team and what each can contribute to making the project work. It is important to discuss the role that people can play. Different thinking skills are necessary to get the results you need. Define the most important elements of the program and then have a short discussion of each to assess priorities. With a list of priorities, define the actions in order of what must happen first, second, etc.

In all cases the purpose is to define the specific actions you need to take.

Step two: the "prevent failure" list

Start working with a clean sheet of paper and define the major complications that could arise to prevent your success. Note this negative thinking is not counterproductive, it is important for your success. Start a list of the three, five or even 10 things that could happen that would stop you from achieving success. Consider:

- What could go wrong and prevent your success.
- Probably won't go wrong but could go wrong.
- Look at your list and rank the most important things that you should plan for and the steps to avoid failure.

You need to identify a shortlist of actions or issues to be completed to stop you from failing in your goal. This is the same as saying, what is the weak link in the chain or our Achilles heel? If you eliminate as many weak links in the chain as possible, your chances of success have greatly increased.

Step three: combine to create your action plan

Your success to-do list many have 10, 20 or even 50 actions in it. Your prevent failure to-do list may have three, five or 10 problem scenarios. Now complete the workshop by combining the most important elements of both lists. Look at all the points on both lists and define the priorities for success. By considering what you need to do to succeed, and what may prevent success, and what you must avoid, the quality of planning will have improved greatly.

Create your own knowledge tools

Many of these tools were created as challenges from past Idea Factory workshops. The value of the results can be extended to your organisation.

The goal of these tools is to provoke new thinking, ideas and solutions. In essence, you want to continually ask, "How does this apply to my/our situation?" The source of the inspiration can come from anywhere. Here are some thoughts on creating your own tools for creating new ideas. I call these "knowledge tools".

A knowledge tool must provoke new thinking

For example, remember this tool? Instead of using the 4Ps of marketing, look at the types of marketing solutions that you would create using the 3Es. Then evaluate the quality, vision and depth of the potential solutions that you achieve. By asking people to discuss things that will entice you inside a business, you may uncover some unique opportunities that competitors will miss.

The seller's perspective	Service view: the buyer's perspective
Price	Entice—How can you entice potential customers to your business or organisation?
Place	Enthuse—How can you enthuse customers to use your services or products?
Product	Excite—How can you excite them to continue to buy your products or services?
Promotion	

The best sources of these tools are articles from industry publication journals, findings from outsider research or simply coming up with your own questions.

Set a general challenge that can be applied in various ways by people within the organisation. Here are some ways to adapt ideas presented in this book:

- The Millennium Challenge: how will factor xyz impact on your business? Your departments? Your people? Your competitors?

- How can we make our clients money? How can we find new ways to add value to clients?

Hints for creating your own knowledge tools

1. Keep them simple. Remember simplicity can be very sophisticated.

2. It must be easy to communicate—one page in length.

3. It should make sense every time you use it.

4. Define your challenges for the business. For example, what are the really big questions that your business must answer in the future. They must provoke new thinking.

5. Read widely to look for insights. Look everywhere, especially outside your industry's rules.

6. Create workshops, meetings or conference themes around the tools.

Your challenge—what are three big questions for your business, group or industry? Turn each into a conversation, workshop or brainstorming meeting.

1. _____

_____

_____

2. _____

_____

_____

3. _____

_____

_____

earning the
title
of being an
innovative
company

part three

6 getting to a result

The goal of every Idea Factory is to get a result. What we consider to be a result can vary tremendously. As the dictionary defines it, a result is the outcome of a process we have used to achieve something. We want it to be a useful outcome; one that provides solutions to our challenges.

Another useful definition of result is that a productive result is one that produces a "decision that provides focus and conviction". There are three key words that need some further explanation:

Decision—The fact is that we must make a decision. Though this sounds obvious, too many meetings, discussions and brainstorming sessions end without a decision being made. With no decision, no action will follow. What does follow is indecision, accompanied by inefficiency, frustration, procrastination and disappointment.

In every decision situation, we should also recognise the do-nothing option. This is not the same as indecision. The do-nothing option is followed when a decision is made not to proceed.

Focus—Whether we refer to our personal or business lives, focus is one of the most powerful weapons we have. With a strong focus on what we want to achieve, we can create a sense of urgency to take the initiative and find the solution.

Conviction—The final aspect is conviction. When you know something is right, you just know. When you have conviction in a decision, you have the fuel necessary to take action and achieve a result. Conviction is perhaps one of the most powerful sources of inspiration that we can harness in ourselves. Without conviction, the greatest ideas will fail to achieve their potential. When this happens everyone loses.

Regardless of the source of your ideas, be it a formal brainstorming session or a lunch meeting with a mentor, focus your attention on adding your energy and passion to the ideas. With a clear focus, use the tools and techniques in this book to continually enhance your ideas and the results you are achieving along the way.

Make the decision that provides a focus for you. At this stage, you may not be sure if the idea will be profitable. However, by allowing yourself to focus on the idea day after day, you will begin to find new ways to build on the basic concept to make it viable and until it is big enough to launch.

Through this process, keep a picture in your mind of the successful business idea in action. Think of it as a puzzle. The picture of a successful business idea in action can then be broken into pieces, much like pieces of a puzzle. In this way you can work on individual pieces of the puzzle and keep the overall picture in your mind (and on paper once you write it down). Every problem or opportunity can be developed in the same way. What is the overall picture you are trying to create? How does it break down into pieces so that you and your team can work on it together yet separately?

When you use this approach, you will find that it will greatly improve your results and solutions in two ways:

1. You work on small pieces of the solution knowing that everything you are doing contributes to the overall success of the project. Therefore even if you only have a spare 15 minutes, you can still add to the project in some small but meaningful way.
2. By focusing on the overall picture, you may identify holes in the puzzle that need to be filled. With any problem or opportunity that you want to develop, it is highly unlikely that you will recognise every piece at first. Acknowledge that there will be

some missing elements. Plan to add more pieces to the overall puzzle that will add value to the solution once you see that something is missing.

Both of these perspectives can greatly add to your success. Suddenly you and your team members can break things into a lot of small pieces and work on them whenever you have a few minutes. You will be able to steal a few minutes here or a few minutes there to add to your future results. You will also avoid the temptation to ignore innovation as something that you can only achieve when you have time.

Hard and soft results

There are two types of results that you can build upon during your workshops:

Hard results—The ideas and plans that you will create. These are very important in the short term as they justify your investment of time and resources. More on this later in this chapter.

Soft results—The understanding of creativity and innovation, the team building, satisfaction and self-esteem gained by staff working on successful ideas. These soft results are probably more important in the long term.

Think of the soft results as being the oil that fuels and lubricates the machines and tools so that you can create and find great ideas. Machines only function without lubricants for so long. As such, learn to recognise and reward both kinds of results. Examples of such soft results are:

- A more positive attitude among staff.
- A general feeling of enthusiasm.
- Staff willing to use new skills.
- A sense of consensus with a willingness to compromise when appropriate.
- More staff willing to raise ideas that they come up with.
- People willing to question things for the benefit of the company.
- People willing to contribute their time and skills to groups to find solutions.

If customers and suppliers are involved with Idea Factory workshops, you can generate the same types of results with them. In the long term, these positive benefits will impact the self-esteem of people. When people feel good about what they do, they contribute and do good work. However, these results will not happen right away. Remember that those with power may not always be the ones with insights and ideas. A receptionist who recognises the voice and name of dozens of customers is as valuable as any research project, as he or she may be able to contribute customer comments and impressions gained from talking to everyone.

Bill Bernbach, a founder of the advertising agency DDB Needham Worldwide, is widely quoted for his provoking thoughts on the essence of creative thinking in business. Before we move to defining what results can be for your organisation, here is a wider perspective on the use of ideas. Give yourself some time to think about your own position and reflect on these comments.

"Is creativity some obscure, esoteric art form? Not on your life. It's the most practical thing a businessperson can employ."

"Merely to let your imagination run riot, to dream unrelated dreams, to indulge in graphic acrobatics and verbal gymnastics is NOT being creative. The creative person has harnessed his imagination."

"We don't ask research to do what it was never meant to do, and that is to get an idea."

"Knowledge is ultimately available to everyone (and every business). Only true intuition, jumping from knowledge to an idea, is yours and yours alone."

With this context, it is clear that ideas and creativity are not related to education, position, experience or expertise. A recent article in the *Harvard Business Review* raised the fact that we can teach managerial techniques such as accounting and operations but we cannot teach the managerial arts of strategy, negotiation and facilitation. We can learn about these arts as you can learn to paint or play music. But we are born with different abilities that may or may not reflect what we actually do in our business lives.

Some people are better with words, music or logic, while others are better at physical activities or personal relationships and understanding. It is a rare person who will be perfect in all of these areas (if any such individual exists at all).

The collective nature of the workshop concept is to capture the skills and experience of people and focus these on a common problem or opportunity. The hard results that we achieve, the ideas and plans we create, will be directly related to our ability to nurture and manage this process; a combination of dreaming and scheming and practical business planning and budgeting.

Focus on the hard results

Though there are countless ways to use an Idea Factory workshop, I will summarise the three types of results that you can expect.

To start with, we find an idea; we see the picture in our mind of what we can achieve. This may be nothing more than a vague notion in your head that starts, "Imagine if we could do something like this...that would be just great for business." If you were writing it down on paper, then you would have a single sentence on the page describing what you see in your head. It could be a better way to service customers, a new colour of paint that you can sell, a new way to manufacture something or a simple solution to a problem.

The story of Sir Isaac Newton is worth repeating. It is said that he was sitting under an apple tree thinking about gravity when he was hit on the head by a falling apple. With that knock, he started on the process of defining the notion of gravity to answer the simple question, why do things fall down—and not up, sideways or in any other direction? He looked at the obvious but chose to question it. With his question, a new body of information was recognised.

The workshop concept is exceptionally good for providing the opportunity for people to think about new things in new ways. Here's an example: your challenge is to find new ideas on selling fruit.

Start with a vague picture in your head with the challenge in mind. Find the first idea that may provide a solution to the challenge of selling more fruit. Perhaps it is door-to-door selling. With this picture of an idea in your head, move to the second stage that expands that into the "opportunity".

Again, imagine the picture of the idea in your mind (people going door to door selling fruit). The second phase tries to figure out what the pieces will be to create the opportunity. No detail at this stage, we simply want to describe the pieces that we can develop later on. For example:

> The motto of big-thinking innovators
>
> **"Wouldn't it be great if..."**

- Start with your one-sentence description of the idea.
- Describe the features of the basic idea.
- How it could work; describe this using simple point form notes.
- What would have to be in place to make it work?
- How could you enhance the idea?
- Are there related revenue sources (or savings) that we can make?

Test your opportunity by then asking:

- Why is it a good idea?
- What is the benefit from your perspective?
- What is the benefit from your organisation's perspective?
- What is the benefit from your customer's (or stakeholder's) perspective?
- Have we developed it enough?

With our example of selling more fruit, here are some of the pieces of the puzzle that would need to be further developed before you can truly evaluate whether this presents a business opportunity.

- For what reason would people want to buy fruit from a door-to-door salesperson?
- How often would they want to buy?
- Is there an opportunity for ordering in advance? How could this order be placed? For example, define low-tech and high-tech approaches.

- How would the person be dressed?
- How could people be enticed to sample the concept?
- What type of packaging would protect the fruit? Is it re-usable? How can value be added through the packaging?
- Is there a business market for the daily delivery of fresh fruit? For example, encourage professional service firms to replace muffins with high-quality fruit for snacks.

As you can see, there are many ways to expand your one-sentence idea into a one-page "opportunity". Don't be too concerned about the practicality of the concept at this stage. You can always cut back; right now you want to be creative and focus on building the ideal solution or opportunity.

In the more traditional jargon, we are defining the vision and setting the goals, and the strategies to achieve this vision. Use the word opportunity for two simple reasons: it is a positive word and we recognise that opportunity is something new and unique that we must create. That means we must do something different to achieve our vision (or the picture of the idea).

Too many strategic plans fail to communicate the vision of the organisation, or its services, products, or the markets that it is trying to create. In fact, many strategic plans are simply business plans that focus on continuing what the organisation does. This approach to planning looks at last year's results and adds some percentage for growth. These plans are full of performance indicators, which attempt to control people through compliance.

Though there is nothing wrong with this approach, start to consider better ways of planning; ones that empower people to use the plan as a document for direction and guidance. Don't allow your strategies to resemble to-do lists. Strategic plans should provide guidance to help you achieve what you intend to become, not just to continue what you already do. Regardless of whether we use the term strategic plan or opportunity, it should outline what you want to achieve in very clear and concise terms.

Time for "Go" or "No Go" decisions

If the product of the Idea Factory is a one-page "opportunity" statement of a new idea that you want to launch, you can now realistically evaluate the costs and benefits of such an idea in both the short and long term. You will have already explored the options and have a strong sense of revenues and expenses of the potential solution. So far, your only investment is time in developing the concept.

This opportunity stage is the time to develop the idea to the point where you can decide whether it is worth pursuing. You should not evaluate the initial idea for one simple reason: you have not expanded the idea enough to explore its value and benefits. You may miss great revenue opportunities simply because they were not obvious. By using the workshop process, the original idea will be viewed, taken apart and rebuilt by a number of different people. In the process the idea will grow into a final concept.

When your organisation becomes skilled at finding ideas, you will be forced to select between them. Do not compare ideas; compare the one-page "opportunities" and you will end up making better decisions. The opportunity stage is the time to consider costs and to compare these costs with other options that you may be facing. In the process you and your team will learn how to add value to ideas, how to evaluate between opportunities and how to continually look for ideas and recognise the bad from the good, and the good from the excellent.

In my first job, we often had to come up with ideas for a wide variety of projects. It was not unusual to raise five or six options after some thought by continually asking, "How else can we do this?" Though it may seem counterproductive to invest time in defining five or six ways to solve the same problem, the result selected often combined the best ideas to produce a superior solution. The first idea was rarely the one selected. By comparing opportunities side by side, it became easy to shape the best opportunity possible by combining elements of various options. Often these opened the door to greater opportunities in the future.

Recognise that you need to separate "thinking" from "doing" and put an equal value on thinking. Do not be in a hurry to start the doing because you use the thinking stage to avoid as many problems as possible that would lead to failure. Avoiding failure is just as important as achieving success in any new venture. Once you are comfortable with your choice of opportunities it is time for the third phase; defining your action plans.

Action plans drive great opportunities

By now you are familiar with the notion of finding insights and turning them into ideas and the opportunities that it will create for your organisation. The last stage is to make it happen. With your insights, it is a basic three-step process:

Find the idea.	*Stage one*
Define the opportunity.	*Stage two*
Develop the action plan.	*Stage three*

There are many ways to create plans that outline the specific actions that you must undertake to complete the project. Many project management books are available on this topic. However you choose to develop your plans, keep them as simple as possible. This includes both the design of the plan and the complexity of the language you use. The goal is to create a plan for action; the actions need management and implementation. The plan guides and directs rather than dictates. Action plans should be clear, simple and concise. You should not have to have a specialist qualification to understand them. They are closely related to our traditional "to do" list—*what do you have to do by when, for how much and with what result?* Don't fill it with lots of jargon that may get misinterpreted by different people.

Use the following case study to follow the progression from ideas to action plans. It is simplified but it will help you to see the key issues. The focus is a new service for the boating industry.

Stage one—finding the million-dollar idea

When you decide to look at a challenge you begin to look at the possibilities of achieving new outcomes. When you do so, you will find new ideas. The result of your workshop could be a one-sentence conclusion that satisfies your challenge, which in this case is to find new business opportunities.

> *Stage one*
> *We will create a new service that specifically targets the boating sector and launch it at our next conference.*

The strength of this one-sentence result is the direction and focus that it gives to all future discussions. You know what you want. You know when you want it. You used a team to find the answer. You will have the team's support in taking this to the next stage.

Stage two—the million-dollar opportunity

The second stage is to turn the idea into an opportunity by creating the plan to make it happen. Many people have commented that they have lots of ideas but can't make them happen. Your challenge needs to clearly outline the idea and the goal for your workshop session— to create the plan, system or strategies to take the idea from a simple suggestion and make it into a "possibility".

The result could be a concise plan of a page or two (unless there is a reason for it to be longer) that provides the main approaches and strategies for turning the idea into an opportunity. For example:

Stage one
We will create a new service that specifically targets the boating sector and launch it at our next conference.

Stage two
To develop our new service for the boating sector, our strategies must include:
1. *Undertake a research program to work with customers to define the key elements of the service (that will differ noticeably from the approach our competitor uses).*
2. *Set up the operational task force to look at the implications and logistics of the new service.*
3. *Define the marketing activities necessary to launch and support the new service.*

Outline of services
- *Our core service will be marketed to small boat producers.*
- *We can enhance our service to add more value to the medium and large producers.*
- *We will use a telephone follow-up approach for the small producers and in-person response teams for the larger suppliers.*

Other possible enhancements
We will look for joint partners, either local or overseas, that we can work with on this service.
In the longer term, we will consider the possible opportunities for exporting the service.

Note that you do not get bogged down with specific detail at this stage. Your goal is to decide whether or not the idea is feasible and how it could be developed into a successful opportunity. Once you see the "possibility", then you can create the specific steps to make it happen. With the strategies in place, they can be costed and assigned or delegated in a co-ordinated fashion. A benefit of this approach is that everyone will know the background to the idea and everyone will feel some ownership of the concept.

Stage three—the million-dollar action plan

The third use of the Idea Factory is to take each strategy (for example, point one above) and create the action "to do" list, complete with cost estimates, deadlines, responsibilities and so on. For example:

Undertake a research program for the boating sector

Stage three				
Action	Objectives	Who	Detail	Time/ Cost
Customer research	Test what is now available and how we can better add value to customers in ways that they will pay for.	EB SS	Ask marketing for list of customers. Develop questionnaire. Use three focus groups (include gifts). Complete report.	Jan 30 Jan 30 $2,500 Feb 28
Create vision for service	Create concise description of the service we want to create.	ST Team	Use recommendations to create "ideal" service. Work to operations to create "realistic" service. Define final service.	March March 1
Testing of proposed service	Research the specific aspects of the services and all costing issues.	EB KT	Use realistic service model to test with several customers for their assessment. Recommendations on final service.	March $500 March 15

This type of chart-form planning framework is often used as it is simple to use and read. You can add columns to make it fit your situation or use the planning approach that works for you. The important point is to get commitment to the plan by involving the right people with its development.

Different types of thinking skills

Are the skills and the thinking different for an architect or a builder? One creates designs while the other creates something from the designs, be this a home, a factory or a skyscraper. The difference in skills and thinking is subtle. Although a stereotype, most people would have a sense of both skills and some would be better at one or the other. All of us have a sense of both skills but probably gain more satisfaction from one than the other. The architect takes pride in creating an idea or vision of something in his or her mind and then bringing that image to life on paper and then in bricks and mortar. The builder most often takes the plans and finds ways, often very artistic ways, to shape a wide variety of building materials into something attractive, useful and satisfying.

Both have a role and neither can exist without the other if both architect and builder are to maximise their business opportunities. However, the ideal relationship between the two extremes of skills and thinking described above is rarely true.

Are you more of a builder or an architect? Some managers are more like builders. They are good administrators and managers but may have little intrinsic sense of how to use an architect's design and concept skills. On the other hand, some managers are architect-type thinkers. At the extreme, both are hard to work for and to work with. The goal is to recognise the type of thinking you prefer, and that of those around you.

If a manager is more like a builder, the staff may feel compromised when they are forced to build a house to satisfy the manager's plan, when they can see in their mind how the house could have been built. That is the plight of the architect thinker: *management may be happy with the results that they wanted but their staff believe that their expectations were too low*. The reverse can also be true; an employee who is a builder, without the inner sense of an architect in terms of design, can immediately pick out the flaws in the detail. The project may be too ambitious or simply a bad technical design. But the visionary manager may be highly frustrated if a great concept gets lost in the details. The soft result in these scenarios is that satisfaction has not been gained.

Obviously, most businesses don't build houses, nor are these stereotypes without their problems. But many ideas for marketing, advertising, special events, sponsorships, promotions or new services were outside the traditional "builder's" tool kit. Many high-quality and often profitable opportunities are left as notes in filing cabinets or at the bottom of a drawer that should be labelled "lost opportunities". Reflect on the past few years and think of the ideas that you left in your "lost opportunities" drawer.

As managers and leaders of business organisations, what are your skills? What skills should you be looking for to balance the overall organisation? We need to find great ideas that lead to great hard and soft results for the long-term success and profitability of our organisations. On the other hand, as architects, what are your skills? Often, these are the people who like to find ideas and get somewhat bored by the time implementation comes around. These people can even be labelled quitters because they do not finish projects. Their true skill is looking at a situation and seeing what is possible or what is missing.

In the end, the source of the idea is not particularly important. Gone are the days when managers were expected to think for everyone in the company. Our move to a faster and more sophisticated business environment will not allow companies that do not allow their staff to contribute ideas and strategies, as well as perform their regular jobs, to survive. This is particularly true for the service sector.

People within a business will have a range of skills and limitations. The astute business leaders will recognise the skills and the potential contribution of people along with their own skills and limitations. With this insight, they will seek to create balanced teams of architects and builders that will create great opportunities.

Your best result is a great opportunity

Here is a checklist of points to consider when considering your results:

- Evaluate the people in your organisation (or your own strengths) to find the strengths that can be harnessed and any that should be added. Some people are designers while other people are builders. Some are a little of both. Consider the mix of people needed to both find the ideas and then implement them.

Original, Creative, Strategic Thinking	Mix of Both Types of Thinking & Experience	Tactical & Practical Thinking
The Insights The Idea	⇒ The Opportunity	⇒ The Action Plan

- There is value in finding experts in both innovative thinking and tactical thinking within a business. Respect both and find employees, customers, suppliers or outside professionals who can provide these skills.

- When you are finding ideas and creating the opportunities, focus on being effective, that is, finding the best solution. Most ideas start with some dreaming and scheming, which generally leads to the ideal solution. It is generally better to reduce somewhat the best solution than to be satisfied with a mediocre solution.
- Sometimes it is best to sit on an idea or opportunity for a day, week or longer as many of the issues that can cause something to fail can be identified and solved.
- Your action plan should focus on "efficiency" once you have a clear vision of what you want to achieve. This builds in effectiveness as the vision clearly directs you to the right actions to take.
- Have your team think through the options before acting. Avoid Murphy's Law that finds that we have lots of time to fix our problems when we rarely find the time to do it right the first time. That's inefficient and ineffective.

The Idea Factory can produce many kinds of results. That magical light bulb can go off inside the head of one of the staff and suddenly you have an idea that sounds great. With that, you enhance the base idea with the features and benefits that will make it work. With a clear picture of the opportunity that you face, you can decide whether to pursue the idea or invest time in other better opportunities. This mix of "architectural" skills and "building and planning" skills then helps to create the very specific action plans that you need to create million-dollar results from million-dollar ideas.

The final test of your results is very simple. When you are in the middle of your action plans and think back to the original vision of what you started off to create or solve, ask yourself, "Does it still make sense?" Don't lose sight of the original challenge of your Idea Factory. Your present actions should contribute to the challenge and this self-review will keep your decisions focused on getting the positive results that you want.

Making good decisions regarding your business problems and opportunities will define how much money you make or how much you save in the process of running your organisation.

Insights
from Chapter Six

- ✪ Innovation is about getting business results. Some will be hard results (such as new ideas that lead to new revenue sources) while others may be soft (such as a stronger sense of teamwork). Both are important results.

- ✪ Not all ideas are the same. Some are seeds of great ideas while others are already fully developed. Recognise the stage of development rather than passing judgement too early.

- ✪ Innovation requires great ideas to be well executed. Pick your best ideas and move these from *ideas* into *opportunities* into *actions*. The framework provides the discipline to get the best results in the end.

- ✪ Recognise the different thinking skills needed to launch new ideas; *original thinking*, *strategic thinking* and *tactical thinking*. Most people can do all three if prompted.

Convert these insights into **action** for your organisation.

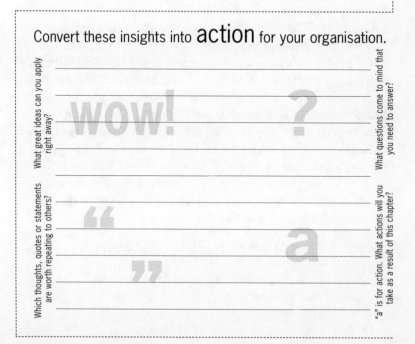

What great ideas can you apply right away?

Which thoughts, quotes or statements are worth repeating to others?

What questions come to mind that you need to answer?

"a" is for action. What actions will you take as a result of this chapter?

7 it's not working very well: troubleshooting the idea factory

The most difficult aspect of adopting an innovation philosophy is that it demands that people start to do new things in new ways. For many, that means they must take some risks. The risk may be to say something that they were criticised for in the past. The risk may be to raise an idea that is laughed at by co-workers. The risk may be to the status that the employee enjoys within the organisation. The risk is that an idea may fail—and no-one wants to be around failures.

We need to reduce the perceived risk of failure. The managing director of a major advertising agency in New Zealand tells of finding a promotional idea for an important client. He raised it with his staff. They thought it was silly and not worth pursuing. He was taken aback by the negativity of his own staff. As the managing director, he did pursue the idea and it was very successful for the client. His very simple idea gained national television coverage. At issue here are several factors that impact on innovative thinking in many organisations. These include:

- Was the idea not particularly good in the first place?
- Was the idea not communicated well?
- Were staff not prepared to be open to the new idea?
- How did they evaluate a new idea?
- Was the criticism justified?
- Could it have been communicated better?

If the idea had not come from the top, it would have been lost. The success that may have been achieved through this new idea and others like it would be replaced with frustration, and less energy and conviction to raise the next good idea.

In most situations, the people raising the ideas will not have the power to move forward with their ideas if others do not support them. This support includes the people at the top of the business. It highlights that those who take the initiative and raise ideas are taking a personal risk that makes them vulnerable. Most people are very uncomfortable when they feel vulnerable.

People need to open themselves up to new ways of thinking to come up with new ideas. To do so, their working environment must be comfortable so they can say things that they think and feel are important. There will always be a tension between feeling vulnerable when raising ideas and the comfort of staying quiet. If the environment is supportive, feelings of vulnerability will dissolve.

The main areas of weakness in any brainstorming or idea-generation session fall into one of two categories:

1. The quantity of ideas being generated is not high.
2. The quality of ideas is not perceived to be high.

The first problem is related to the poor implementation of the systems, while the second is related to the lack of tools, training or outside perspectives to bring out the ideas that are innovative and useful.

The quantity of ideas is not high

Symptoms of the first problem will include:

- Ideas are not being generated during the workshop.
- Workshops seem to have little energy and people seem to have little enthusiasm.
- Getting people to focus on the issues or contribute to them is difficult.
- People do not feel the workshops are worth the time.
- People are not trained to come up with ideas.
- There is a degree of scepticism among staff.

Solutions to these issues will relate to the set-up, structure and facilitation of the workshop. It is crucial to review the steps you took in setting up the workshops and how you involved the team.

Set-up and structure

Nothing can happen without preparation. Ensure that the time necessary to undertake the workshops is actually available to the team involved. Does it force them to work overtime to complete their regular work? Talk to the group, preferably one on one, to find out what they feel to be the issue. The time could be wrong or the place may not support the workshops.

The other element that hinders success relates to poorly written Challenges. Does the team actually believe them to be worthy of their time? Many organisations call a brainstorming meeting to talk about the future of the company yet the issues seem so basic that most people turn off very quickly. Do they have real information to look at such issues as sales, new markets and job security? And if, after spending 90 or so minutes talking about these issues, no new thinking, consensus or decisions are reached, the perception that the time was not well invested is reinforced.

The purpose of the Challenge is to get agreement that the workshop is worthy of a serious investment in time and worthwhile to prepare. Test your Challenge statements with team members to get their support. Modify it if necessary to get the results.

Facilitation

The person leading the session need not necessarily be the boss. In fact, this may be one of the problems. If the "boss" is always the leader, this may undermine the results for the following reasons:

- The person at the top may not actively listen to the suggestions being made. Likewise, staff may continue to be inhibited and avoid raising ideas with the boss because they don't believe that they will be heard.
- The skill of facilitating and leadership should be shared for others to develop. This also gives people a sense of ownership

of the concept. Some of the biggest critics can become the best supporters by their active involvement.

- The person at the top may also be missing an important perspective by not allowing someone else to take over the workshop. From the floor you may recognise why is it not working or how it can be enhanced through training, different team members and so on.
- An outsider, perhaps a consultant, professor or a business adviser, can also be used to ensure the collaborative effort of the entire team is focused on the same agenda. The facilitator's role is to be a referee to keep opposing viewpoints from ruining the exercise. They need to encourage people to recognise their own biases and respect the opinions of others.
- The facilitator also acts as a coach to get the best thinking from the group members. There is a fine balance between encouraging people to think harder and being insulting. We want people to be challenged to think hard.

Quality of the results is not high

The second significant issue is the quality of the ideas. Any judgement on the quality of ideas is both a perception and a reality. The perception reflects the amount of new thinking, creative energy and results that people contribute that lead to some feeling of accomplishment. The reality is the expectation of the potential results that can be achieved, in terms of the value, profit opportunities and other technical components of the ideas. In some cases, the "perceived" results will outweigh the value of the actual results. The issue of raising the quality of ideas is far more challenging than raising the quantity of ideas.

In general, there is no one way to do this. Improvements in the quality of ideas will reflect concerns of training, a well-defined Challenge statement, the time invested in preparation by participants, the make-up of the team and the facilitation. Each contributes to the success of new ideas but no one element in itself is enough.

Training for creativity

Many people are not comfortable with brainstorming. Many do not really understand how it works. There are numerous options for training programs in this area; look for courses that seek to give people insights into their own abilities to think and solve problems.

The virtue of training has been demonstrated many times over by people such as Dr Edward de Bono. People can learn skills to be more creative in their approaches to problems and opportunities. Some of the programs offer a tool kit approach such as de Bono's Six Thinking Hats model. In this case, every imaginary hat requires people to take a different perspective on a situation. The objective is to use such tools to give people the experience of looking at new possibilities in a way that is encouraging and safe. The Six Thinking Hats system separates the different types of thinking; emotion from fact, positive from negative and critical from creative:

Does Innovation Training Pay Off?

The INNOVATION NETWORK in the USA recently reported on a study on the Return on Investment on creativity in comparison to Total Quality Management initiatives and R&D investments. Though the sample is small, the results are very indicative.

- Federal Express gained a 200 per cent ROI.
- United Technologies gained a 600 per cent ROI.

Creativity programs can impact on all facets of a business that enables the business overall to be more effective.

1. The Red Hat signifies feelings, hunches and intuition.
2. The White Hat calls for information known or needed.
3. The Yellow Hat symbolises brightness and optimism.
4. The Green Hat focuses on creativity: the possibilities, alternatives and new ideas.
5. The Black Hat is judgement, the devil's advocate or why something may not work.
6. The Blue Hat is used to manage the thinking process.

Other forms of training attempt to re-open people's creativity through exposure to new perspectives. This highly personal form of development attempts to give people the confidence to use their intuition and ideas. They help people to be more involved with the process and to become passionate about the opportunity of creating new ideas.

However, it must be recognised that creativity training is much like athletic training. No matter how many workshops on fitness and health you attend, and no matter how expensive the running shoes are, if the knowledge and tools are not used, nothing will be accomplished. As with physical fitness, the more you get involved, the better you become and the more you enjoy it. For most people, it becomes easier and more satisfying.

It may also be useful to provide people with a greater understanding of the industry or the business itself. Do not assume that all people understand the business or how it makes money. Simply by giving people this knowledge may focus their thinking on the key issues.

The Challenge and preparation

The objective of the Challenge is to define the specific issues that will lead to a solution or an opportunity. Talk to those involved to assess how useful the Challenge is for preparing their thoughts and ideas. Put an expectation on the preparation. Tell people to spend 15 minutes, an hour or whatever to think about the issues. If some team members do not prepare while others do, it creates the potential for an "us and them" atmosphere. Look at the Challenge to decide if it adequately prepared the team for the workshop.

Team make-up

Look at the people involved. If you have others to consider, look at the mix of skills and personalities. Key questions:

- Is there a bad apple that is spoiling the workshop?
- Is someone dominating the discussion?
- Do people trust each other to be open with their ideas?
- Are the people skilful and knowledgeable enough to contribute?
- Should you involve an outsider to add some skills and some prestige to the event; perhaps a consultant, customer or supplier who is a good brainstormer?

Do not force someone to participate if they really are not interested. Some people may be better at solving existing problems while others like to create new opportunities. The selection of people, as with any business or sports team, is very important to your success. Select the people carefully and look for the specialty skills that will make a difference. There are many resources available to provide insights on selecting of people and building teams.

Facilitation of the group

Make a careful assessment as to the skills of a facilitator. They do not need to have the answers, but they do need to know how to ask questions, how to listen, how to recognise the good ideas and how to capture the key points. It may be best to select a few people who seem to enjoy this role and develop their skills. Resist the temptation for the boss to always be in charge. Any attempt to change the rules that were created by the boss may be too challenging for team members.

One way to deal with this is to use an outside professional facilitator for the first couple of sessions. This may help to get people comfortable and familiar with the potential outcomes and processes. Select one who will also help to train people in the process.

To make the Idea Factory work, two over-riding factors need to be in place to succeed:

1. Commitment from the top

There needs to be a commitment from the very top of the company to give people the time and resources to participate in workshops or brainstorming meetings. In fact, the executive and managers at the top of the company need to be involved with such workshops themselves. This sends a powerful message to the organisation that ideas and innovation are an important part of the company's future. There is also an element of giving people the power to make their own decisions wherever innovative thinking is needed.

2. Complimentary and supportive company policies

Related management policies such as reward systems, training, recruitment and promotional opportunities must be consistent with the philosophies not just of innovation but also good management principles for the future.

Keep in mind that every organisation has formal rules (written contracts, procedures and manuals) and informal rules (the implicit rules that are not written down but that everyone has learned, based on the actions of managers and supervisors). What is the impact of these rules on the way people act? Be aware that staff generally have a very different perception than many managers may want to acknowledge. The point is that the staff's perception is their reality. If they believe that the Idea Factory is just another fad, then that is how it will end; on a pile of old management fad books and manuals.

In any change program, it is best to start thinking small; tackle a challenge that is small enough to handle yet real to the business. Start with something that is positive and important for people yet not so complicated that results will get bogged down in old arguments and power and politics.

Groups or teams of people can work through tremendous differences in age, education, culture and experience providing that they have a will to do so. Many of the traditional team-building exercises can help to make people friendlier to each other but they may not actually find the ideas that will make the company more profitable and jobs more secure.

One useful approach to start is some form of climate survey; that is, a survey of staff attitudes to get their feelings toward the company, its managers and its future. The findings of such staff attitude surveys can pinpoint problem areas long before you launch the program. For example, if people are cynical about the benefits of being innovative, they will not respond.

From research on teamwork, one interesting fact that keeps appearing relates to the success that groups have and their ability to work together. Success and results can bind a team better than any number of team-building exercises. These exercises have their place but a workshop that requires people to work together on a common goal, in which contributions are sought, listened to and used, and that results in something useful that the team believes to be of value, is a very powerful glue to bind people together. Anything that prevents this from happening will contribute to a lesser result. If teams are not working well, too much energy gets spent on the process and dealing with conflicts rather than enhancing ideas and opportunities.

The workshop may not fail but instead of scoring an A+ on the idea, perhaps gets a B or C score. We teach our children to study and prepare to get the best results in school. Preparation is equally necessary for innovative thinkers to maximise the results they achieve. The difference in business between an A+ and a C– could be thousands or millions of dollars of potential earnings, more secure jobs and a more profitable future.

One test that you can use to measure the quality of the results you are achieving is to have everyone grade the result from your workshop. From their perspective, ask two questions:

> **Is your organisation open to innovative thinking?**
>
> WAVE™ is one of several diagnostic tools developed to measure the innovation capabilities of organisations. WAVE™ measures:
>
> 1. The extent to which business strategy, structure and culture provides an environment that allows and encourages breakthrough thinking.
>
> 2. The mindset and the expectations of managers and technical specialists.
>
> 3. Whether a company has the right skills and processes in the right places to achieve breakthrough.
>
> www.waveglobal.com

1. Does the result reflect our best effort to find a solution or opportunity? How could we have improved the way we worked together to achieve the result?
2. Do you believe that the potential of the problem or opportunity was fully explored and developed? How could we have had a better or stronger result?

The answers could be very revealing. Both are important and reflect different issues.

Some brainstorming workshops end with most people being satisfied that they achieved a good result. However, one or two may feel that something is missing. They may have tried to have raised a point that was not considered which they believe could have led to a stronger result. Be aware of the signals. People may have insights that could create new thinking on the issue. These people often work hard to consider a wide range of options or perspectives on a problem or opportunities. As such, their contribution comes from a different way of viewing the problem. They may be alone in their thinking on a subject.

Perhaps the first and most important place to start is to talk with the people involved. These discussions may reveal issues important to understanding what hinders the flow of new thinking and ideas. As with any philosophy on business, there are no guaranteed rules that will apply to all companies. You must adopt and adapt to make them fit your organisation and the specific people and opportunities that you face.

Here are a series of suggestions, points and tips from experience with Idea Factories that refer to the Golden Rules. They provide examples of the approaches, guidance and leadership necessary for successful innovation.

1. Listen to people

Listen to people when they comment, criticise, offer suggestions or ask questions. Respond positively.

- If you look at any staff attitude survey, one of the probable outcomes will be "managers don't listen to us". Use an internal staff attitude survey, discussion group or one-on-one interviews to gauge whether staff perceive that they are being listened to. Also, in this process ask about any issues that may prevent success; the risks that people may face if they succeed or fail.
- Managers may not listen for a number of reasons. Some may believe that it may threaten their jobs if staff have too many good ideas. This is a serious issue in many older organisations in which managers grew up in a system of top-down decision making. Suddenly having to deal with ideas floating up from the bottom may be very unsettling.
- If you get easily upset by criticism...deal with it. Your staff and customers should not be forced to cope with your problems.

- Never assume that you know more than your staff. Your staff can talk to customers and get useful insights. Your consultants can talk to customers and get useful insights. Remember that many of today's frustrated middle managers are tomorrow's consultants. It is cheaper to pay for their ideas as "staff" rather than wait to pay them consulting rates.
- There is a belief that for every customer who complains about your service or product, another nine stay silent. The same probably applies to staff. Don't silence the one who dares to speak out. Don't ask someone to put something in writing before you will act on it.
- Read books on customer service for tips on getting feedback. A lack of feedback from staff and customers can be a sign of excellent service or it can be a sign of withdrawal. People have resigned in their own minds and they are waiting for the right opportunity to leave. It creates complacency.
- Learn to understand where staff or customer anger and frustration comes from. The passion comes from a deep sense of injustice or pride; harness this for your own good. Too many people leave jobs when they outgrow their current responsibilities and management either fails to recognise this or fails to provide enough of a challenge to keep the person. Either way, good skills may walk out the door with your company secrets.

2. Seek out ideas people

Seek out employees, suppliers, customers and others who are ideas people.

- Who do you hire? Some people hire people who think exactly as they do. Some people hire people who will challenge their established ways. Have you really defined the type of people, skills and personal attributes that will make your business successful in the future?
- What is the mix of "architects" and "builders" in your organisation in terms of the style of thinking? Write this into future job descriptions.

- Promote the fact that your staff and customers have lots of great ideas; this will help to attract future staff who are feeling alienated in their own organisations. A motivated new staff member who comes with lots of knowledge of the competition contributes vital new energy!
- When hiring, ask about leadership roles people have held in volunteer associations, schools or other organisations. You may find that this experience is very valuable to your business.
- Develop a network of customers who can contribute a wide variety of perspectives. If you prefer, start with an outside research or consulting company to facilitate this action. Many businesses find great value in a customer advisory panel.

Work with accountants and lawyers who can help develop ideas. An hour or two of their time could be very useful as they bring in a wider business perspective. If they can't provide ideas, change your advisers!

3. Respect ideas

Support and respect ideas that are generated. Give credit where and when it is due.

- When someone finds a new idea, who gets the credit? How management handles this issue will dictate the success of any innovation initiatives.
- If a top executive in a workshop claims an idea that the team believes was a group idea, the concept will die. Retain the integrity of the ideas and the results that are produced.
- Be positive about good and bad ideas. If the quality of idea is poor or average, consider the skills that may be missing on the team. A bad idea may be useful from a learning perspective. It may take a few bad ideas before you find a million-dollar one!
- Continually remind the team of its importance and recognise the results openly within the business.
- Remember that some people cannot communicate very well. Don't miss the point that they are trying to make. It might be very good.

4. Be committed

Be committed to the process of finding ideas for the ongoing success of your organisation and its people.

- Be committed to the process and find ways to demonstrate your commitment.
- That means take a long-term perspective; develop a year-long plan.
- Start with proper training to get people comfortable with innovation processes. Find out if they want more information. Before you will get great ideas, people need to have the skills and the tools.
- Talk about the need for ideas whenever possible. Encourage people to do likewise. Use your regular team briefs, staff newsletters or bulletin boards to promote the new ideas that have been generated.
- The quality of the ideas will reflect people's understanding of the process and their involvement with it. In other words, they must know what they are doing and have the time to do it— plan regular workshops and stick to it!

5. Give ideas

Give ideas generously to others—knowing that you will be rewarded in turn.

- Some people actually feel offended when you give them an idea. They think you are being critical. Recognise that just as you may have had to risk presenting your idea to them, it may feel like a risk on their part to accept it. Know that you will quickly gain the trust of those who do appreciate your initiative.
- Offer to work with (or have your best ideas people work with) suppliers or customers to brainstorm ideas for their business. This can build relationships and potential new business for everyone involved.
- The best company is one that makes its customers successful. Involve your customers in your innovative efforts. This is an excellent way to build a relationship with them.

The Idea Factory's Golden Rules are designed to provide guidance for creating the company policies and rules, both formal and informal. When you review the way your company works, start by placing the rules on a page and look at the policies to see which help or hinder ideas and innovation. All company policies must stand up to these critical factors:

1. **Listen to people**—Are staff actually encouraged to comment, criticise, offer suggestions and ask questions? Does the management team live up to this challenge on a day-to-day basis?
2. **Seek out ideas people**—Does the company seek out people with ideas; those that offer something beyond the traditional job responsibilities?
3. **Respect ideas**—Are ideas respected and rewarded?
4. **Be committed**—Do the company's plans demonstrate a commitment to innovation and problem-solving? Does it set targets and have a plan for "new ideas" for the year? If so, are enough resources (staff time, facilities, money) given to finding ideas to generate million-dollar ideas?

There are always two perspectives that are important to consider: that of the manager or management team, and that of staff. Their responses may be similar or they may vary widely. Explore the differences in opinion. If the responses differ, you have discovered something extremely useful for the profitable use of innovation. Your goal is to focus on finding million-dollar ideas. It may take some time to get there but the trip will be worth it. The only true long-term source of new ideas is the people within the company.

Insights
from Chapter Seven

- No-one said being innovative is easy—but is it harder than being mediocre?
- The main weakness for all innovation processes fall into one of two categories:
  1. The quantity of ideas being generated is not high.
  2. The quality of ideas is not perceived to be high.
- The first problem relates to poor implementation of the systems, while the second relates to the lack of tools, training or outside perspectives to bring out the ideas that are innovative and useful.

Convert these insights into **action** for your organisation.

What great ideas can you apply right away?

Which thoughts, quotes or statements are worth repeating to others?

What questions come to mind that you need to answer?

"a" is for action. What actions will you take as a result of this chapter?

building your idea factory: 8

a place for innovative thinking

Up to this point, we have talked about the Idea Factory as a program for innovation. For many organisations, the program extends to setting aside a place within the business for creating opportunities. This may be a room specially designed for creative thinking or a section of an office or lunchroom. The room dimensions are less important than creating a space that is specifically designated for creating opportunities and finding those million-dollar ideas.

Establishing a permanent Idea Factory is much like opening a company fitness gymnasium. It should be managed in a similar way. The benefits of a work force that is healthy, fit and alert are obvious. But getting people to start some form of fitness program can be very challenging. Thinking of the Idea Factory as a mental gymnasium is a useful way to review some important points:

- Creativity, like fitness, is not a "special event" or something that is only done at a yearly retreat. It must happen on a regular basis to produce great results.
- The best equipment and training are needed to maximise the benefits to be gained from the investment.
- Coaching and one-on-one training can greatly improve the results by providing timely advice, motivation and the assurance that a course of action will lead to positive results.

One of the many benefits of having a specific space for creating opportunities is that it sends a powerful signal that the business is interested in new ideas. Making a space for innovation will create a lot of initial interest in the concept. You can launch it, give it an official name and develop a plan for its ongoing use.

Innovative thinking is important

There are three key things people will look for to gauge whether management is taking innovation seriously:

1. Creating some space and time for creativity.
2. Allocating a budget for equipment, training and related resources.
3. Creating an agenda or program to focus on creating opportunities for the company.

With these three in place, your Idea Factory will have a much greater chance of success. To start with, allocating space for innovation means that the business is serious about its investment in innovation. For most businesses, this space has a cost (although in practice it is often reclaimed from an unused work room or storage room).

The Creativity and Innovation Lab at Polaroid Corporation reclaimed a small section of a much bigger, century-old building in Cambridge, Massachusetts. Within the walls of the old building, two significant tenants did much of their research and invention for which we must be grateful.

- Alexander Graham Bell moved to the building in the 1880s to finalise modifications for the telephone. Though much of the work started in Brantford, Canada, he completed the actual development of the telephone and made one of the world's first telephone calls to his assistant, Mr Watson, from the site.
- Edwin Land spent much of the 1940s working on the proto-types of a camera system that would allow for instant photographs. He succeeded in his efforts and created Polaroid Corporation, which grew to a work force of 20,000 at its prime. It is said that Land would get so excited when he made a breakthrough discovery that he would run recklessly out the door of the building and on to the street—often into the path of

an on-coming car. The company built a barrier on the sidewalk to force him to run around it before running onto the street. It was hoped that he might notice if a car was coming.

Though it is unlikely that many buildings exist with such a long and rich history of invention, research any such advantages your facilities may offer. Companies are using facilities ranging from old storage rooms to abandoned churches for planning and innovation centres.

A permanent space creates a focus on innovation. Much like a beacon or lighthouse, it continually reminds staff that innovative thinking is important and that it is taken seriously. By being visible, people see the room or the space, wonder about it, question it and get comfortable with the idea that it is a permanent part of the new way of working.

Even those who will be critical of an innovation lab or Idea Factory (or any other name you choose to call your facility) can be useful. Their criticism will raise the topic for discussion. Good leadership will be able to convince them of the benefits of the space. The arguments they raise will also suggest some of the key impediments that will hinder the acceptance of these processes. It will also pinpoint the staff members who become excited by the potential for a facility in which it is allowable to raise opinions and explore new ideas without risk. People working within companies that have set aside a space for brainstorming recognise that it can be a safe zone for thinking.

The Polaroid Innovation Lab was a positive example for the company when it opened. One of the co-founders, Suzanne Merritt, says, "It sent a powerful message that the company—which is very dependent on a continual source of new product innovations—was open for thinking."

Focus on shaping opportunities

The space that you set aside must be used for one thing: to create opportunities for the business. Though the Idea Factory often talks of the need to solve the ongoing problems of the business, every activity that takes place in the space must focus on creating a positive long-term opportunity.

The problems that need to be addressed by your company must be framed in a way that converts them into some form of creative process. The difference is subtle but very important. Do not disguise attempts to create efficiencies by cutting back or reducing expenses as an opportunity for employees to be creative. The focus of all efforts must be positive and aimed at creating the future. The space can be used to create opportunities, improve systems and find new ways of being more effective. If you do not honour this distinction, the space will not produce the results that you want. In the same way as you would not use the gymnasium to force staff to ride bicycles that power your machines, do not use the innovation space for fixing management errors of the past.

Integrity is a vital component of innovation. As your Idea Factory begins to capture ideas, sort them into categories so you can recognise the different types of ideas that come up. Some will be more immediately valuable than others will. Here are some suggestions for sorting them into four different types of idea bins:

The Recycle Bin
You've had these ideas before, but forgotten them. Something brings them to mind. These could also be ideas you don't need but could pass on to someone else.

The Loony Bin
These are the crazy ideas. They are outrageous and will never work. On the other hand, if you could find a way to make them happen, it would be a breakthrough. Store loony ideas here and keep thinking about how they could become possible.

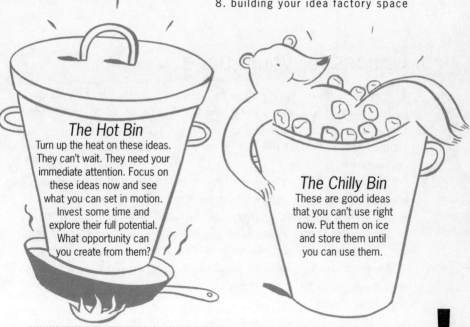

The Hot Bin

Turn up the heat on these ideas.
They can't wait. They need your
immediate attention. Focus on
these ideas now and see
what you can set in motion.
Invest some time and
explore their full potential.
What opportunity can
you create from them?

The Chilly Bin

These are good ideas
that you can't use right
now. Put them on ice
and store them until
you can use them.

INSIGHTS INTO IN-HOUSE CREATIVITY CENTRES

In-house creativity or innovation centres fall into two categories. Some are
designed for scientists and technologists involved with R&D. However, most
lead innovative thinking in a much wider sense within their organisations.
For example, the *Creativity & Team Centre* at Eastman Chemical Company in Tennessee
seeks to improve the corporation's creative processes. Some of the full time facilities
include the Polaroid Corporation *Creativity Lab* in Boston, Lucent Technologies *IdeaVerse*
in Chicago, the Nortel Networks *Design Interpretive* (with its 20 year history) and the
3M *Innovation Learning Centre* in Utah. As with all corporate initiatives, they depend
on executive commitment, which can vary impacting on the life span of the centre.

These centres launch training programs, idea generating sessions and actions to
raise the profile of creativity through publications and presentations. In many cases,
scientists and engineers use these creativity labs to find solutions to technical
problems that have alluded them. Often the result is found by applying a different
problem solving technique that leads to a new conclusion.

In Australia Bristol-Myers Squibb recently opened the *Innovation and Learning Centre*
to ensure that innovation becomes an integral part of the culture. Its activities include
ideation techniques to give employees the tools to approach problems differently.

Aside from the *mindwerx Idea Factory* in Melbourne, a range of overseas consultants
offer idea generation centres including the *THINKubator* in Chicago, Doug Hall's
Eureka Mansion in Cincinnati, PriceWaterhouseCoopers *Idea Zone* in Philadelphia
and the Cap Gemini Ernst & Young *Centre for Business Innovation* in Boston.

Options for your space

The most common approach is to dedicate a room for the purpose of being an Idea Factory. It should be able to fit up to 15 people (depending upon the size of the business) comfortably around some tables. The secret to the design of the room is that it must be comfortable.

If possible, find a room that has a view of something inspiring, such as a park, the ocean or just open space. Giving people a chance to relax their eyes and focus on the distance often contributes to a better environment. Views have also been shown to reduce stress levels in people. Stress is generally not a contributor to innovation.

In some cases, corporate furniture is shipped out and replaced with more informal sofas, tables and chairs. Some people bring in their own chairs.

Businesses that cannot dedicate a complete room often set aside a designated space in a large room. This allows for posters to be put up and sofas to be moved in so that people can sit facing each other. In these cases, ensure that others in the room will not be upset by the noise of the enthusiastic discussions that will become commonplace.

Another option that some businesses are using is a temporary site for innovation by taking over the boardroom for a week or using a near by facility. One organisation does its brainstorming in an old church for inspiration. Places like museums, planetariums or even a public school may offer a unique setting for a specific type of challenge that you face. This portable or temporary approach attempts to get the benefits of managing premium-priced space but allows for the benefits of the space for the days or weeks that it is needed. Regardless of the option you choose, remember that it sends a powerful message. The leaders of the organisation must lead by example. If you want staff to use the facility, you must use it as well.

Equipment for an Idea Factory

Equipment such as flip charts, white boards, paper and a bucket of various coloured markers and pens are standard for every Idea Factory. These are the tools of creativity. However, along with these standard tools, think of things that aid creative thinking for your organisation. Some of the following aids are useful as prompts for thinking:

- Building-block toys are useful to get people relaxed and modelling things with their hands.
- Puzzles and thinking games (even children's games) are great for stirring people's imagination.
- A wide range of colour photographs can prompt new ways of viewing a situation. Some people laminate these photographs, which may feature nature, people, unusual products or simply things that are interesting to look at.
- A collection of rocks, pieces of wood and other elements of nature can be used for seeing what has been ignored for years.
- Music that sets a mood works for many groups. Music, like the visual arts, creates a positive environment that can stimulate creative thinking.

Do not be concerned with looking unbusinesslike. This is nonsense if your facility is achieving results. However, keep in mind that some people work best surrounded by funny hats, toys and colourful posters while others prefer a simple, uncluttered environment. The only rule here is to decide what will work best in your environment.

Related to equipment is the range of support materials that are available. There are numerous books, magazines, posters and guides available on innovation and creativity. Look for information in business magazines and copy articles to key people (or post them on your bulletin boards).

Build in a recognition system

To continue the successful use of the space, it is necessary to recognise the achievements that are made. Often these may seem small but they start a line of thinking that leads to great achievements. After all, the most significant action plans start with a single thought.

Create a wall of fame or achievement for the centre. Show the person's name, a picture and describe the achievement. Create an approach that fits with the culture of the company and one that supports people in the daily use of innovative approaches for creating opportunities and finding quality solutions to important problems.

Managing the space

The Idea Factory is a workshop setting, not a meeting room. It can be used for training as long as the training is related to creativity and innovation. A functioning Idea Factory will be used regularly to offer training on creativity and problem-solving tools as well as for workshops designed to find new ideas through brainstorming. This may involve individuals or groups. Have someone manage the facility who is willing to be a champion for innovation within the business. They should have specific experience or training in this field and also have credibility within the organisation. This could be someone from training, marketing or the top management team. There job is to manage the overall innovation strategy and ensure the facility is being used for training and idea generation work that leads to new solutions or opportunities.

If the space becomes a haven for creative thinking, people will leave their desks or work area to go there for 10 minutes, 30 minutes or more to work on a specific issue. Just being in the room will put them in a positive frame of mind for thinking about new and useful solutions to their challenges. Individual brainstorming is a powerful measure of the Idea Factory's success. More formal workshops should also take place regularly to ensure that your business is getting the positive results that it needs.

Once again leadership is critical.

If the CEO is seen to be using the Idea Factory to think through a business decision, it sends a powerful message to everyone in the company. Research on organisations that are highly innovative finds that these implicit messages are critical for the success of innovation programs. These messages become the stories of the company. These stories either endorse the company's interest in creative solutions or make a mockery of it.

For the stories to support innovation, the key decision-makers in the company must take the initiative to use the facilities and be seen to be doing so. Creating space for an Idea Factory is a signal of change that can lead to a powerful force within the business, based on the principles in this book.

However, it starts with leadership.

HOW TO SET UP YOUR INNOVATION CENTRE

Here are some specific tips for planning your Idea Factory:

- Designate a physical space for the purpose of creative thinking.

- Make it highly visible and announce when it is "open for thinking". Have a party or reception to open it. State the company's intentions for the room and innovation in general.

- Make it available to everyone in the organisation for the purpose of thinking or innovation, not just those perceived as having responsibility for being creative (such as marketing and new product development). Making our accounting and production systems innovative is very important.

- Create a playful, relaxed environment with furniture and props. Ask people to bring things from home that are engaging and entertaining.

- Recognise and reward teams for frequent use of the space.

- Keep a visitors' logbook that includes team members' best ideas from each session and other interesting highlights.

- Have disposable cameras in the room so each team takes photos of their session. Create wall space to display photos of creative teams at work. Change the photos often.

- Create a "Great Ideas" wall. Post ideas that are not needed at present for future use, or to be adopted by another team on a different project. One company calls this the refrigerator, in which they store great ideas until needed. You can also sort your ideas into bins: hot bins, loony bins, chilly bins and recycle bins.

- Build the Idea Factory's reputation as a place where surprising, thought-provoking things happen. Have a lunch guest each month to stimulate thinking on a controversial topic.

- Collect and post inspiring quotations about creativity and innovation. Change these on a regular basis.

- Circulate articles about creativity and innovation through the company, stamp them with your Idea Factory logo or name so it is visible. Promote the fact that the Idea Factory is developing resources on behalf of the company. Encourage others to send articles, websites, books and tapes to the Idea Factory.

- Arrange demonstrations or classes on unusual topics such as drawing or mythology. Lessons learned are personally inspiring and can be applied in later creativity sessions on work-related topics.

- Let people use the space for personal creative projects. The more activity in the space the better. For example, a group of scientists formed a band at Polaroid that practised in the "lab" weekly.

- Invite guests from other companies to visit the space and participate in sessions. This creates a sense of pride in the achievements that are being made and recognises the contribution being made by the innovators in the business.

For the Idea Factory facility, see www.ideafactory.com.au for details.

Insights
from Chapter Eight

✪ The Idea Factory can be a room or a space within the business that is set aside specifically for creating opportunities.

✪ The space may be designed for creative thinking. It sends a signal that innovative thinking is important and it becomes a safe place to think big.

✪ The room dimensions are less important than creating a space within the building that is specifically designated for creating opportunities and finding those million-dollar ideas. What can you create in your organisation?

Convert these insights into **action** for your organisation.

What great ideas can you apply right away?

Which thoughts, quotes or statements are worth repeating to others?

What questions come to mind that you need to answer?

"a" is for action. What actions will you take as a result of this chapter?

9 creating your strategy for innovation

To compete by being innovative is not to compete in the traditional ways of doing business.

Rosebeth Moss Kanter, former editor of the *Harvard Business Review*, told an Inc. Magazine conference I attended, "The secret of innovation is that it gives you a temporary monopoly. It means that you can charge more for it."

That's a pretty good reason to consider the benefits of nurturing innovative thinking in your organisation! To compete through innovation is to continually look for new advantages in the services and products that you deliver, and in the business's ability to continually create new advantages. When you do so, you create a competitive advantage that is unique to your company. In this way, you compete by not competing directly with competitors, and you create a monopoly in terms of your ability to generate unique ideas.

When you create a business advantage in your market you are less vulnerable when unfavourable economic, currency or other negative changes occur. In fact, if you are able to create such changes, they will have a negative impact on your competitors. To compete through innovation initiated from well-developed ideas from people within your business is a much stronger asset than any technology, tariff barrier or form of protectionism. The philosophy necessary to create this advantage is hard to appreciate for managers who are used to managing in an environment where the status quo, as defined by the traditional industry rules, somehow turn into laws which can not be broken. To ensure that policies are put in place to support innovative thinking and the opportunities that this will create, it is necessary to build commitment to innovation through a simple yet complete "innovation strategy".

As outlined in the opening of this book, the concept of an innovation strategy does not yet exist in a formal sense. Many businesses will have some elements of such a strategy, as many companies had elements of marketing years before it was recognised as a focus critical to business success. What shape an innovation strategy will take in the future will be dictated by the successes and failures of the companies that lead the way today.

The innovation strategy has, at its base, the notion that we tend to achieve what we focus on. It has been said, "We find the right idea for the right solution at the right time." When we focus on finding a solution to a problem or creating an opportunity we tend to get a result. Based on this simple notion, you can create an innovation strategy to direct the development of solutions to a few, well-selected problems and opportunities.

The concept of what an "innovation" strategy could look like is very intriguing. It may be easier to talk about what it should not be for a moment.

- It should not be linked to technology unless new technology is needed to create growth in some way, or to solve a particular problem. Your objective is look at the problem before you jump to the perceived solution. Technology often deals with the symptoms of problems, not the actual problem.
- It should not be linked to training unless the need for specific skills for people's growth drives the training. Secondly, these skills must be focused on achieving specific outcomes.
- It should not be linked to marketing unless it is linked to the targeting of new markets, the provision of new services and products, and processes to achieve both.
- It should not be linked to any one specific area unless the objective is to make the entire business function more "innovative" in terms of the ways it creates new opportunities.

What an innovation strategy should look like is a creative exercise in itself. As soon as you define the parameters of such a plan and work out a formula, it suddenly loses the significance to your company. Matrixes and formulae that become popular in the business media should serve as guidelines only. A business wanting to be innovative, regardless of its size and scope, must start to shape a strategy that is designed and created by the people in the business, rather than by outsiders.

The innovation strategy needs to be created and written to establish:

1. An agenda for action based on defining the particular problems and opportunities that, if satisfied, could lead to growth or some advantage.

2. Any necessary change in business processes to encourage communication, listening, sharing of ideas to make the environment more open to more innovative thinking.

3. Training needs in concept development skills, brainstorming, planning, team work, etc.

The first objective creates the framework and structure that you can follow. The second objective recognises the importance of people. An organisation's people are the source of the fuel that will drive innovative thinking. It is necessary to ensure that sufficient time and resources are spent on developing both objectives. Having an agenda for innovation without considering the processes used to create innovation will not create a lasting advantage to the business. It may provide a temporary advantage. Focusing on the processes of innovation without defining the specific actions to work on provides little benefit as the energy within the business that could be nurtured and harnessed will be wasted.

When such a strategy is in place it is measurable and a budget can be justified in a normal planning sense. The need for such a strategy is not limited to the size of a company. Most entrepreneurial companies have a strong sense of creating opportunities. The source of the ideas behind these opportunities can be created as a result of applying your resources in any number of ways that make sense for the business. You may:

- Use a team workshop to solve a major delivery problem that customers have highlighted.
- Sit by yourself to find a way to target a particular market, using the disciplines of brainstorming.
- Host a series of customer panels to discuss a new service or product range that you want to create.

In each case, the single-minded focus on achieving a result helps to create the reality. That reality must be defined in your overall innovation strategy.

If you prefer, think of the innovation strategy as a spotlight that focuses on a particular "spot" long enough to isolate the issue—and give people the time to find a solution. The spotlight will not illuminate the entire company; only the portion in need of focus. But this does not exclude the many small improvements and enhancements that can be made.

To convert the Idea Factory workshops into a significant benefit, you must line up potential problems (that are in need of a solution) and potential opportunities that can benefit from the focus of a concentrated spotlight. You cannot solve every problem nor create every opportunity at once. It is foolish to waste resources trying to do so. However, what you can do is to attack each one with a systematic approach that strives to achieve several things:

1. To identify the range of potential problems that must be addressed and the opportunities that can be created. This is a creative exercise in itself to broaden the discussions of the important issues for the business.
2. To define the priorities of these organisational problems and opportunities in terms of the financial and organisational importance to the business (or other criteria which you believe are important). This may include a range of objective financial measures and subjective management measures.
3. To create the time and the tools for individuals and teams to actively seek high-quality solutions to these issues for the long-term success of the business.
4. To focus on improving the ability to solve problems and to create opportunities. Hence, it is important to continually examine the process and the results.

Any organisation that maximises these strategies or business philosophies will achieve success. Not only is a focus placed on reducing expenses and increasing revenues, an equal focus is placed on improving your ability to do so! That is a tremendous result for any organisation, be that a not-for-profit agency looking to raise the awareness of a particular disease or a multinational company looking to expand its markets. It is a very simple approach to business and one that is very empowering for the leadership of the business and staff.

Following are several ways to make innovation a reality in your organisation.

1. Set a year-long series of challenges

Starting with your strategic plans or your yearly business plans as a base, consider the important business challenges that will add most to the bottom line of the organisation. They can range from any aspect of the business as long as it is important and relevant to the people involved.

Anyone who has taken the most basic accounting, economics or finance course will recognise equations such as this. In the context of the modern knowledge and service-based industries, it is worth reconsidering some of the basic terms.

$$\text{Rate of Return} = \frac{\text{Revenues} - \text{Expenses}}{\text{Equity Invested in the Business}}$$

No longer is the application of the traditional definition as it applies to the investment in bricks, machinery and property of much use when the new currency of many businesses is based on ideas, knowledge and experience. The following discussion is not intended to be critical of the traditional accounting definitions, rather to expand upon the concepts for modern service-driven business in which the assets that produce value have less to do with bricks and machinery and more to do with brains and initiative.

Rate of return—Traditionally, the meaning given involves a financial return for the money invested in a business. For many of today's professionals, home office workers, owners of small and medium sized businesses, the rate of return is not strictly a financial calculation. It must also reflect security, lifestyle, peace of mind, flexibility and other personal priorities of the business owners and the employees. A powerful discussion to have within a team or a business is the definition of "return". What is important to different people with the organisation? The financial returns will always be important, but the long-term capacity to create value and wealth is not always measured by today's results.

Equity invested in a business—One of the most significant changes in business growth in most developed countries is the explosion of micro businesses. These two-person, 10-person or 50-person companies are often capable of tremendous profitability and growth. But the traditional definition of equity was the amount of cash invested in the business. If a business is launched with a concept for a service and Rolodex of business cards, what has been invested? The traditional measures would suggest very little. The knowledge economy would suggest that there is tremendous value in the contacts, experience and potential solutions that someone is capable of delivering. However, most small to medium companies start with the well-known type of equity—"sweat" equity. In the end, for an entrepreneur or innovator the true measure of a return on equity is whether the profits justify the amount of cash, energy and time that was invested in the business concept. Also, they will look at the degree of stress, pressure and lifestyle changes that were necessary as well. All of these factors need to be considered when we start to look at the concept of equity and the return that is earned from this investment.

Increasing your revenues

How you view revenues must also include some discussion of the type of customers you want to service, the amount of challenge or learning that you want, the travel, perks and other benefits that add value. Revenues can also be defined in terms of acquiring new assets or resources. A proposal to a supplier for an exchange through barter of services or product may save resources that can be invested into another type of project. Revenues can also be defined in terms of benefits gained for your customers that result in goodwill or the enhancement of your branding or image.

Managing your expenses

Expenses not only include financial costs, they also include time, stress and our other limited resources. There are many stories of executives who walk away from careers because they did not balance the costs of achieving their health, emotional, spiritual, financial and career goals.

The smaller the business, the greater the influence of the non-financial aspects of these definitions. It is a worthwhile exercise to discuss these issues within your company, to create your own common understanding and language.

Creating your agenda

One of the first outcomes for the Idea Factory workshops must be to create a list of significant challenges to define:

1. Growth opportunities that you can create or develop that will add value to your business and impact positively on revenues. There is a second component to this section—one of the opportunities you list should be undefined for the moment. It is the opportunity that will arise in a month or in six months. Not every significant opportunity can be defined upfront. Allow for a "blank" opportunity that you can fill in at a later date. This is critical to ensure that some funding is available for future opportunities.
2. Significant problems that you need to solve to improve your business. Generally, these will be to decrease expenses or manage expenses more effectively.

Note that you will be going against the trend in many organisations. It seems that we have virtually become fixated on putting all our time into finding efficiencies. Most of our business publications offer techniques to cut back, save more or reduce. That's fine, but recognise the simple truth that you can also increase your return by increasing revenues. Research is coming forward to suggest that companies that put too much effort in downsizing and outsourcing staff went too far. By eliminating too many people they also cut out the soul of the company.

By identifying a total of four to eight major challenges—and committing to the process of meeting these challenges—you will come up with ideas that can make a significant difference to your long-term success. Use your first in-house workshops to define a year-long action plan to increase your revenues and decrease your expenses. Plan today to start each activity with similar workshops to expand the project.

2. Establish your priorities

It is important to separate the exercise of creating opportunities from selecting them. All too often good ideas fail to be recognised as they are judged too early. This is one of the critical rules for brain-storming. Also remember to convert your ideas into opportunities before you evaluate them. Here are some considerations to consider when reviewing your lists:

How to evaluate problems

Problems cost money. They add to inefficiency in terms of lost productivity, extra product repairs, extra time needed to deal with complaints, lost customers, bad will, rework, re-inspection, warrant claims, administration, discounts and so on. Problems also have another cost in terms of the frustration levels of staff who get fed up with fighting fires to solve immediate problems. Many will say they have seen it all before. When you look at problems, consider the total number of customers and staff who are affected by the problem.

You must attempt to put a cost on these factors. You are trying to measure the cost of not fixing the problem. How many customers will be lost? How much staff time will be spent on fixing the same problems? How many $$$ will be spent trying to fix up the problems? All these costs are inefficient and non-productive. When we actually look at the cost of not fixing our problems, fixing them suddenly becomes urgent.

In the service sector, many problems in our organisations come from the design of our systems and processes. Most costs that are wasted in service businesses reflect:

1. Business systems or processes that don't work the way they were designed (*or were never designed properly in the first place*).
2. Activities and money spent on the wrong techniques or solutions to fix the problems.
3. Complicated systems or processes that can simplified by removing the non value-adding activities. Often, we do things for historical reasons, not because our customers necessarily benefit from them.

Perhaps it is better to consider it this way—by not fixing a problem, you are investing your capital, time and energy in your problems. What is the cost of this investment?

Once you can calculate a cost of not fixing the problem (*even a basic assessment is enough*), you can then think about the amount of time and money you could have spent on creating a new opportunity rather than wasting it on "unfixed" problems.

Side by side look at problems and opportunities

Many people say, "We look at all problems as opportunities." Though this is an honourable way to view problems, there are some differences. For a start, a problem already exists while an opportunity is something waiting to happen! Here are a few points to help you take advantage of the differences.

	Solving problems	*Developing opportunities*
Typical example	"Customers complain of a billing problem. We need to fix it."	"A customer said we should consider a new service that she, and numerous others, could benefit from and pay for!"

	Solving problems	Developing opportunities
Key questions to ask	Did the problem arise from a poorly defined system? If so, you must also fix your organisation's systems that creates these problems or allows it to happen. Why you didn't notice it before?	What are competitors planning? Are they tackling opportunities better than you are? Is your business changing? Where will your future revenues come from?
Key issues	The problem tends to be well-defined or at least definable. Easier to research as you can ask specific questions about customers' or staff's experience with the problem. As you get closer to a solution, you can be more targeted in your research. As you advance, the options tend to narrow to a single cost-effective solution.	The opportunity is likely to have lots of options or ways to be developed. Hard to define the "best" opportunities. Hard to research when something does not exist. Must use intuition and foresight as a guide. More risk is involved with something new than something that is copied. Greater opportunities exist for growth as the impact can spread over all customers.
Risk factor	Generally little risk as the problem already exists. Customers have waited for some time for you to notice. Doing nothing is the biggest risk—customers or staff may walk away.	Risk of the unknown. The numbers of options tend to add risks. Personal risk to key people if it fails and the management and culture of the business do not support the risk-takers.
Potential long-term benefits	Solve the problem and tell customers you have listened to them. They will appreciate this.	Continue to impress old and new customers with new services. Being a leader is what many customers now expect of their suppliers. Can greatly enhance team-building within the business.

How to evaluate opportunities

Any opportunity will take time and money to develop. The key to using the Idea Factory concept is to make a lot of small investments of time or money—an hour every week, a workshop every month and perhaps a day-long review every year. As well as the financial side of creating an opportunity, the other issue to consider is the effect on you and your staff when you do something new: it's exciting! Everyone loves doing new things and if you use the themes in this book, the reward will be there.

Also, consider the "opportunity cost"—the financial and other benefits that were lost because the opportunity was not developed. For example, if you had taken the opportunity to build a trade show booth and attended a couple of major shows, what is the value of sales that you could have made? What is the value of being perceived by the staff as being interested in new ideas and creating opportunities? What is the impact on motivation levels? Add up this total to measure the opportunity cost of not taking the action. Though it sounds impossible to calculate, you should consider these facts. To create a sense of urgency in your organisation about creating new opportunities, use these factors:

- How much could you have made if an opportunity had been developed?
- How much staff time was spent to continue the status quo rather than invested in creating new opportunities that could lead to new revenue sources for the business?
- How many customers did staff not impress or gain, as you did not take the initiative?

The cost of lost opportunities would be staggering for many organisations. Consider for yourself how often you have experiences with minor lost opportunities:

- The number of times you went into a restaurant and would have ordered an extra drink had a waiter asked?
- The number of times you have ordered something only to find out that it was out of stock?
- The number of times that you had to call a business because of a busy telephone line or an incompetent receptionist or sales person? Secondly, the number of times you gave up and went to a competitor?

All these examples were wasted opportunities for the business involved and yet management was not even aware of the lost business. These ideas may sound negative (and most accountants would not support the approach) but they are real for people who work with ideas. Often, opportunities are not created because no-one takes the time to develop them. It can take an outside view to recognise the potential in something.

The other issue to consider is a budget to provide the costs of developing opportunities. In effect, you are attempting to budget for something that does not yet exist. The only fact is that the cost of your staff is already budgeted for. However, some businesses now provide a budget for ideas that have not yet been identified to avoid a lot of unnecessary negotiating about funding when ideas arise during the year. It is more efficient to set aside some funds to develop ideas and empower staff to use them to create the concepts rather than invest their time in finding sources of funds.

How to set priorities

Two important points for setting your priorities for an innovation strategy:

1. The sooner you solve a problem that is bleeding your organisation of resources, the sooner you benefit by saving resources that can go into other opportunities that actually create resources.
2. The sooner you start a revenue or value-adding opportunity, the sooner you benefit by gaining new resources.

Does this sound basic? It is that simple. There is always a cost in terms of time and resources in taking action and in not taking action. We must start to measure the cost of not taking action. Too many businesses stagnate and wither from the disease called "status quo".

Another factor to consider is the nature of the problem or opportunity. Is it long term or short term? Clearly, any problem that has been a "problem" for a long time will have a significant benefit when fixed. Place your emphasis on such problems. Similarly, any opportunities that permanently add to your resources should be the priority.

Judging your options

It's impossible to predict which ideas will succeed. The selection of the best options to pursue begins and ends with your ability to recognise a great idea when it is staring at you. Although we attempt to measure the potential financial returns of new opportunities, we must also recognise the number of assumptions that go into these forecasts. The most sophisticated forecasts can only attempt to predict the future. From research and experience, we combine this analytical process with our judgement to make the go or no go decision on a new opportunity.

One of the exercises often used to help people to identify good ideas is to create a personal definition of a "great idea". What are the attributes of the last really great idea you had or heard?

- What did it feel like?
- What did it look like?
- What did it allow you to do?

Make up your own definition so you have a clear idea of what you are looking for. *"A really great idea is one that..."*

Sir Geoffrey Palmer, former Prime Minister of New Zealand, responded to a challenge to define a great idea when he said, "Analysis and thought are critical to the recognition of a great idea, but they are not enough. They are a necessary condition, not a sufficient condition. In the end, good ideas often come from instinctive flashes of insight. But when you have a good idea you know it with conviction, even if other people do not recognise it."

Analysis, thought, insight and conviction. These are powerful words. If you want a definition of what an innovative business does, it could be one that harnesses the analysis, thought, insight and conviction of everyone in the entire organisation and understands how to focus it for the benefit of customers and staff. Sir Geoffrey Palmer also defined a second interesting feature of a great idea: "One important feature of good ideas consists of having a gift or ability to see how things may turn out, how parts of the future may unfold."

That's a powerful vision for a business that focuses its people on innovation. To be able to see how parts of the future may unfold is a highly valuable asset.

What does your analysis, thought, insight and conviction suggest are the best options for your business?

Insights
from Chapter Nine

✪ How can you break the rules by out-thinking your competitors? This is the essence of innovation in organisations.

✪ Create your innovation strategy (include a page in your yearly strategic plans) to focus on the problems that need to be solved and the opportunities that need to be kick-started into life!

✪ Use this list to shape your timetable for the year.

Convert these insights into **action** for your organisation.

What great ideas can you apply right away?

Which thoughts, quotes or statements are worth repeating to others?

What questions come to mind that you need to answer?

"a" is for action. What actions will you take as a result of this chapter?

10 give credit to the source of your growth: people

Giving credit where and when it is due is a significant challenge for many business executives. If you are successful in the pursuit of new ideas, exactly who owns the million-dollar idea?

In a sporting context, when a player does something spectacular he or she is rewarded by team members and coaches. Professional athletes also get media interviews, bonuses and endorsement opportunities. The astute coach not only recognises the athlete who scores; he also recognises the players who created the scoring opportunity. Often, a superb defensive play at the opposite end of the field can lead to the brilliant result.

With the Idea Factory, who owns a million-dollar idea? Who owns the profits of a million-dollar idea? Who decides what the rewards should be and how they should be shared? The answers to these questions will dictate the success of an innovation program.

What motivates an idea person? It is a complete fallacy to believe that money motivates all people. It may. It may not. Money is often only one factor; the job may be simply a means to an end.

For many people, being creative leads to a powerful feeling of self-worth. When we allow people to think about problems and opportunities and then acknowledge the results of their efforts, the result is a sense of empowerment. People want their creative efforts to be acknowledged and appreciated. When this happens, something interesting occurs.

Anyone who is physically active recognises a special feeling when he or she finishes a walk or workout. Physical changes happen within the body to bring on a sense of satisfaction. Though there are numerous physiological explanations for this, suffice to say there is a high from being active. Some call it the "runner's high". When we experience creativity, there is a similar feeling of satisfaction and accomplishment. The intrinsic "creative high" is very real for people.

There is a special type of motivation that begins to drive creativity within people—the need for the creativity high! It is very similar to the runner's high. Once you experience it, it begins to be a desire. For some athletes, the high can become an addiction but it need not be this extreme. However, recognise the power of creativity and help people to focus their ideas for the betterment of the organisation. This is a natural extension of a quality innovation program.

People get a tremendous sense of satisfaction when working through a process of finding ideas, developing them, helping with the implementation and finally, sitting back to see the results.

This sense of satisfaction is a very strong motivator to do it again. As the cycle is repeated, the ideas tend to get better and often bigger. The benefits to any organisation or a group of motivated idea generators and implementers are very obvious.

For many people the sense of excitement and wonder also translates to their personal lives. Innovation may be a business strategy but the source of creativity is a very personal experience.

The implications for management policies should be clear. If they are conceived to encourage and support the various philosophies in this book, people will respond. People's past experience of offering new ideas will dictate the speed of the response. In many cases, we find people who have simply given up. They are on a holding pattern until they find a new job. As such, many dollars are spent on salaries and training people who are willing to switch to a competitor who offers a better opportunity for long-term employment.

A similar argument is made for the significant growth in home-based businesses. If you research the reasons why people left their organisations to set up their own businesses, it tends to reflect one of two concerns:

- Their ideas and expertise outgrow the business. In other words, they stop being challenged by the organisation.
- They have become too frustrated by the lack of contribution that they are able to make to the organisation's decisions and success.

This situation is compounded by today's shift from manufacturing to the service and knowledge industries.

People with one, two or three university degrees are much less willing to adapt to organisations that do not offer opportunities for growth and satisfaction. For many people, money is not the sole motivator. It is much broader and harder to explain what creates employee satisfaction.

We often hear of the importance of the marketing concept of "brand equity". It describes the need to continually focus on ways to enhance the perception of a brand's products and services. However, we do not put the same emphasis on creating an equivalent concept involving its people, or perhaps "people equity".

We know about the strength of brands such as Coke, McDonalds, Ford and IBM. But how many organisations are known for being great companies to work for? The emphasis placed on creating great "marketing brands" is rarely matched by that placed on creating great company to work for.

Allowing people to be more creative in their everyday work can help build this equity. A key to this is leadership and it applies equally to not-for-profit agencies and profit-based businesses.

Though many people have followed a similar philosophy, the founder and director of a New Zealand company puts it very well. Bruce McIntyre, who started sewing backpacks and outdoor adventure gear in the garage of his parents' house, has built a large company whose products are now available in many countries. He believes that "our job is to create organisations in which people can actually contribute to the success of the business".

Fundamental to this belief is his notion of reconsidering how we manage our businesses. He expresses his dismay at the extensive use of the term "human resources" to describe our "people" management. "People are not a resource; they are the source," McIntyre says. "People are the source of ideas, energy and all the things we need to make our organisations successful in achieving their objectives."

If we don't respect that fact, we will fail to build innovative organisations that continually seek out profitable value-adding opportunities. Your management programs must respect that people want to feel a sense of fairness in exchange for their contribution to the success of the organisation.

However, too many radical changes in organisations can lead to employees becoming sceptical. People have seen too many change programs that did not respect their contribution. They lacked integrity. People did not commit to its success.

Building an innovative organisation will not guarantee your success. However, there is much evidence to support the contention that innovative organisations have a much better chance for success for these critical reasons:

- Innovative companies find better, long-term solutions to their problems. This frees up resources to concentrate on activities that add value to the business rather than stopping unnecessary expenses.
- Innovative companies seek and find better long-term business opportunities. In the process of doing so, people are more willing to put in the hard work, knowing that positive results and rewards will be generated.
- Innovative companies tackle the challenges of tomorrow, next year and the next decade as there is a long-term commitment to the organisation, its customers, employees, products and services.

Despite these positive attributes, there is still no guarantee that innovative thinking will result in a successful business. However, we boost the odds of being successful and staying in business in the future.

Ideas and innovation are very powerful tools for business growth. Being an innovator is a title that you earn from the employees, customers and the wider business community. Business decision-makers can greatly contribute to this success by creating environments that support people as the "source" of their success.

To conclude, it is important to revisit the Golden Rules for building innovative organisations:

1. Listen to people

Listen to people when they comment, criticise, offer suggestions or ask questions. Respond positively.

2. Seek out ideas people

Seek out employees, suppliers, customers and others who are ideas people.

3. Respect ideas

Support and respect ideas that are generated. Give credit where and when it is due.

4. Be committed

Be committed to the process of finding ideas for the ongoing success of your organisation and its people.

5. Give ideas

Give ideas generously to others. You will be rewarded in turn.

Innovation and creativity is a powerful philosophy for achieving business growth. Is it the next fad? No, not at all. It is a rediscovery of the energy, passion and excitement that created many businesses in the first place. Ironically, many of today's most creativity-stifling organisations often had highly innovative founders. It is necessary to rediscover the insights that created your organisation.

Focus on developing the skills of finding and managing ideas at all levels of the organisation. Shape the culture of the organisation to be open to new thinking. Ensure that leaders support innovative thinking through their everyday decisions.

Companies must rediscover people's inherent ability to contribute to their organisation's success. Being creative in one's business life and in one's personal life is not a luxury limited to a few people—it is a genius that our organisations must nurture and reward. If thousands of businesses begin to focus on improving their bottom line by empowering staff to actually use their curiosity, expertise and intuition, thousands and thousands of new ideas will be generated.

Many of these will lead to breakthrough products and services which will be created or enhanced to improve our lives.

The same conviction must apply to not-for-profit organisations as well. The more innovative their use of limited resources to service their stakeholders, the better our world can be. But it starts with one business at a time. It starts with one manager at a time. It starts with a single decision—the decision to ask some tough questions:

- How can we make this better?
- What's missing here that adds value?
- What's good enough but could be better?
- Which industry rules could we break to be noticeably different?

When we ask these questions, we will find exciting answers. People have all the potential to find the solutions. When companies open the doors to their own Idea Factories, they will find the solutions and create the opportunity that leads to both personal and business growth.

"Creating business growth through ideas and innovation."
—Ed Bernacki

That's more than just a slogan. It's the philosophy and strategy that successful companies of today use to ensure that their tomorrow will be profitable and rewarding.

Insights
from Chapter Ten

- ✪ Reward and recognition fuel innovative thinking that leads to new ideas. Money is just one element. Often the ability to continue to work on an idea is a powerful motivation.
- ✪ People are the source of all new ideas. They provide the energy to create value but too many businesses misunderstand how to harness this creative potential.
- ✪ Your efforts must focus on the challenges at hand. Keep one eye focused on present day issues while the other focuses on longer-term issues. Anything short of this will not maximise the opportunities we face.

Convert these insights into **action** for your organisation.

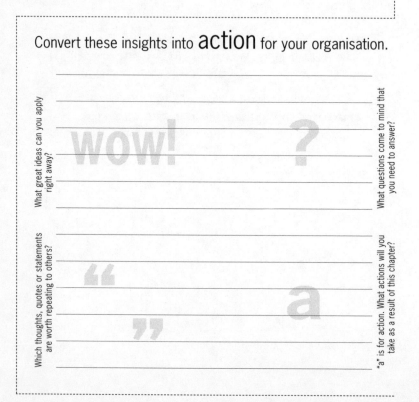

What great ideas can you apply right away?

Which thoughts, quotes or statements are worth repeating to others?

What questions come to mind that you need to answer?

"a" is for action. What actions will you take as a result of this chapter?

appendix
innovation
strategy
framework

Create your innovation strategy now!

Even your greatest ideas will not survive if they are thrown into a hostile environment. Regardless of your position in the organisation, be a leader in shaping an environment to nurture ideas and to support the people that find them. Revisit the ideas presented in this book to shape your own innovation strategy. It must focus on two key elements:

1. The problems that can be solved and the opportunities that can be developed that will make a difference to you and your organisation. This reflects the "innovations" in which you will invest time and resources.
2. The training, processes and resources necessary to ensure that the way you develop ideas is also innovative. Your processes must be as innovative as the innovations you want to produce.

The innovation strategy is designed to focus on the new initiatives that you will invest. It is as important as your marketing, people management or operations strategies. Here are five key elements that should be part of an innovation strategy.

1. Overall objectives for innovation

The main objective is to shape a more innovative organisation; that is, an organisation that is capable of harnessing the best thinking in the business on the challenges it faces. An innovation audit can also provide powerful insights for guiding the specific objectives. Your objectives should focus on developing the overall capability to innovate, rather than any specific innovations. An important element of setting the overall objectives is getting a sound background to the issues that will enhance and hinder your opportunities for success. Begin with a survey such as that found at www.waveglobal.com to guide your future decisions.

2. Communicating innovation

Every change of management process requires a major communication effort to inform, educate and enthuse people. What are the specific actions you are to take? You can use presentations, posters, team meetings, in-house newsletters, Intranets, bulletin boards and individual training sessions to communicate your message. One of the key roles for management is to continually reinforce the importance of communication and to lead the way by being seen to participate in the process.

3. The challenges to tackle

For each year, define the specific projects that will be undertaken (acknowledging that new or more important problems or opportunities may arise during the year). Use them to set the timing for new developments. For example, start with this: "To create our strategic agenda we will focus on these areas (problems to solve, opportunities to create)"...See the details below on creating a planning framework to help you act on the challenges you face.

4. Training for idea management

People need skills to manage ideas. Do they know how to brainstorm? Do they need help with team building? Presentation and facilitation skills are also very useful. Also, consider employing outside speakers (including your clients and suppliers) who can contribute new perspectives to the challenges the business faces.

5. Measures of success

Review the section of this book on hard and soft results. Both are important. You must solve the problems well and create robust new opportunities. Continue to monitor staff understanding and attitudes toward this process.

In summary, your innovation strategy will fit into the overall strategic plan for the business. It should include these components:

1. A range of problems that must be addressed and the opportunities that can be created (including space for an opportunity that has yet to be identified). These will be assessed in terms of a set of priorities defined in terms of the financial and organisational importance to the business (or other criteria which you believe is important).
2. An agenda to manage the mechanics of the innovation work (the allocation of people, time, the tools, timing of workshops, resources and training). This will include the element of a review to continually examine the innovation process and the results.

Within the context of the plan, the agenda may only require a page or two of notes under the headings of:

- Opportunities to Develop—these generally create the potential for new revenue streams.
- Problems to Address—these generally save resources that were spent on errors and poor processes.

Create the space for involvement

With your priorities in place, the focus shifts to translating the plans into a timetable for action. This requires a schedule and a realistic assessment of the time, space and resources you need to achieve the results. Show it to your team. Get their commitment to a year-long challenge to make the organisation more successful (and hence, their jobs more secure). Because you can't do everything at once, make this a year-long project but plan today to start each activity with similar workshops to expand the project. The long-term benefit can be tremendous. You focus on problems rather than jumping between them.

In some cases, you will recognise that outside assistance may be necessary to complete the project. The type of chart below will assist with your identification of any skills or manpower necessary to complete the challenge.

Key expense reduction opportunities	Timing for start of actions	Potential benefit	Project leader, team & leader
1. Implement re-use and reduce program	March	$20,000	GNP–BE
2. Overhaul invoice billing systems	June	$10,000	IS
3. Simplify purchasing system to reduce time requirements	November	$35,000	ED

Key revenue generation opportunities	Timing for start of actions	Potential benefit	Project leader, team & leader
4. Develop new trade show presentation and strategy	April	$20,000	GNP–BE
5. Develop new service option for existing customers	July	$10,000	IS
6. Develop export strategy for product line XYZ	November	$35,000	ED

Create your "Idea" production plan

Establish Your Idea Factory Workshop Schedule based on the month you will deal with the particular problem or opportunity. Set specific dates and plan for each event by ensuring that all of the proper resources, research and background preparation is completed and available for the specific dates. If you plan to include outside specialists you should invite them to participate as soon as possible.

1. List the main problems in order of importance. Decide when you will deal with each and prepare the challenge.
2. List the main opportunities you will create this year in order of the greatest impact they will have on your organisation.
3. Draw a line across to indicate in which month you will tackle each challenge. This simple form of visual planning quickly highlights any scheduling problems.

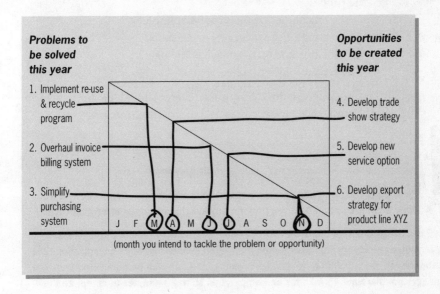

Build in reviews of the process

It is important to focus on *improving* the skills and abilities of people to solve their own problems and to create their own opportunities. It is important to continually examine the process and the results. Every meeting, planning exercise or action involves a process. One of the most powerful aspects of innovation is the continual focus on making improvements to the processes of creative thinking and problem-solving. As people begin to work together and achieve results, the skills will be become stronger and more powerful.

A simple review process can be used to discuss the processes people use to work together. This is not an exercise in being critical of what may or may not have happened, it is an exercise in taking a constructive look at the process to see what, if anything, was missing. For example:

1. Were some specific skills missing? Would training help or is there a need for a specialist to become involved?
2. Were any resources missing that could have helped—market research, background and so on?
3. Were any decision-makers missing who should have been part of the process?
4. Were the mechanics of the process suitable?
   - The timing of the meetings or sessions?
   - The location or offices used as the base?
   - The technology or facilities?

The outcome of this continual review should be finding more effective and efficient processes to execute the strategies.

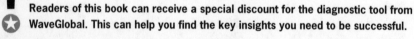

UNDERSTANDING YOUR ORGANISATION'S READINESS FOR INNOVATION

Readers of this book can receive a special discount for the diagnostic tool from WaveGlobal. This can help you find the key insights you need to be successful.

WAVE is a diagnostic tool that uses two questionnaires, one for senior managers and one for other employees, to measure the innovation capabilities of an organisation. The questionnaires are supplied to respondents online, and can also be completed on paper. Managers need around 45 minutes and employees 15 to 20 minutes to complete the questionnaires. There is also a data sheet that is usually completed by a manager from the organisation. WAVE's most distinctive feature is the six-factor model it uses to present data on the complex subject of business and organisational innovation.

To find out how this powerful tool can help your organisation, see www.waveglobal.com

To find out about the special pricing package for readers of *Wow! That's a great idea!* email info@ideafactory.com.au

Get the language right

The final shape and presentation is less important than the results it helps you achieve. George Orwell, the author of books such as *1984*, wrote an interesting essay called "The Politics of the English Language". It contains a number of rules for good writing. The best recommendation is to keep it simple and clear. People who are involved with the process must understand the plan quickly. Simplicity is the key. There are two important lessons that can be learned from Orwell's essay.

First, when creating your innovation strategy, your use of words is very important to the overall understanding that people will have of the plan. Orwell suggests that we follow these rules to produce effective writing:

1. Never use a figure of speech that you're used to seeing in print.
2. Never use a long word when a short one will do.
3. If it's possible to cut out a word always cut it out.
4. Never use the passive voice where you can use the active.
5. Never use a foreign phrase, a scientific word or jargon if you can use an everyday English equivalent.
6. Break any of these rules rather than say anything outright barbarous.

Orwell's fifth recommendation focuses on eliminating business jargon. Do not use words such as paradigm shift, BPR, CRM or any other jargon.

Second, to paraphrase Orwell's sixth point, break any of the recommendations in this chapter rather than produce anything outright barbarous. If you believe that your ideas and approach will produce a higher quality innovation strategy, then use it. Successful innovation strategies will be produced when people look at the perspectives in this book and use their analysis, insight and conviction to create innovation strategies that are meaningful to the people in their business. Always keep in mind that innovation only happens when we act on our ideas.

Worksheet

Create your innovation strategy

1. Overall objectives for innovation:

_____

_____

_____

_____

2. Actions for communicating innovation:

_____

_____

_____

_____

3. The challenges to tackle:

_____

_____

_____

_____

4. Training for idea management:

_____

_____

_____

_____

5. Measures of success:

_____

_____

_____

_____

get your conference
navigator guide

Think of the last conference you attended...*did you make notes and never look at them again*? If so, you need a Conference Navigator Guide.

The Conference Navigator Guides helps you find more and bigger ideas at the conference, and then shows you how to convert your ideas into actions back at work. The Guides replace the pad of paper you get at a conference with a fun yet serious 60-page idea journal. Each page is designed to encourage participants to listen for ideas and act on them. Pages include:

"Once in a while a new idea surfaces that makes me wonder...

"Why didn't I think of that?"

George Gendron, editor of *Inc.* Magazine said this about the Conference Navigator Guides. *Inc.* Magazine used the Navigator at all of its conferences in 1998.

- Assess your past participation.
- What is a great idea?
- Where do great ideas come from?
- How to pick your workshops.
- Active listening to different types of speakers.
- Active note taking.
- Swapping ideas with others.
- Mingle mingle—how to network.
- Taking the great ideas home.
- Turning ideas into actions.

Plus...30 pages for notes and a place to insert business cards of important contacts people make.

Send me a Conference Navigator Guide!

No. of guides _____ × $29.95 = Total $_____

Shipping $2.50 in Australia, $5.00 internationally $_____

(GST inclusive) Total payment $_____

Send your cheque to:
The Idea Factory, GPO Box 1074J, Melbourne, Victoria, Australia 3001

Name _____

Company _____

Address _____

City _____ State _____ Country _____ Postal code _____

Email _____

hosting your
own idea factory

The Idea Factory offers powerful idea generating workshops to help your organisation find big ideas that solve problems and create new opportunities!

These are designed to achieve specific results such as:

- Develop new service concepts.
- Create new marketing approaches and strategies.
- Identify the top challenges your organisation faces.
- Solve specific client problems in powerful new ways.

These "Idea Factories" often take place in Melbourne at the **mind***werx* **Idea Factory**. It is a place for brainstorming new opportunities for business, not-for-profit and public sector organisations.

Ed Bernacki started The Idea Factory Concept in 1996 to create a greater sense of urgency for businesses to be more innovative. He has worked with many organisations to find powerful new ideas using a process that is empowering and productive.

He is an international speaker, writer and adviser on the use of innovation and creativity in business. He has spoken at numerous conferences in Canada, the USA, New Zealand and Australia including several prestigious conferences organised by *Inc.* Magazine in the USA. He has been widely published in management and marketing magazines.

What are your big challenges?

The Idea Factory could be the perfect way to solve your major challenges. For further information contact:

Wow! The Idea Factory
GPO Box 1074J, Melbourne, Victoria, Australia 3001

Web   www.ideafactory.com.au
Email   wow@ideafactory.com.au
Telephone within Australia 0412 608 940
              international +61 412 608 940

wow!

that's a

great idea!

An ideal corporate gift for your team, customers or suppliers!

This book will give your team, or your customers or suppliers a tremendous resource for finding new and powerful ideas to make their business more innovative and effective.

To order extra copies, use this form or email your request to wow@ideafactory.com.au Individual orders are $29.95 (plus shipping of $2.50 within Australia or $5.00 internationally).

For a larger order, you will receive a major discount

- For 5–10 copies, your investment is $25.00 per copy (plus $2.50 shipping).
- For 11–25 copies, your investment is $22.50 per copy (plus $5.00 shipping). You also receive for FREE, a copy of Ed Bernacki's Conference Navigator Guide, a $29.95 value.
- For 26 or more, your investment is $20.00 per copy (plus $8.00 shipping). Your also receive for FREE, a copy of Ed Bernacki's Conference Navigator Guide, a $29.95 value plus a set of set of posters to accompany the book, a $39.95 value.
- For orders over 100 books, email wow@ideafactory.com.au

Send me more wow! that's a great idea! books!

Send this page and your cheque to:
The Idea Factory, GPO Box 1074J, Melbourne, Victoria, Australia 3001.
(If you prefer use a separate sheet of paper.)

No. of books _____ × cost per book _____ = Total $ _____

(GST inclusive)   Shipping $ _____

                                               Total payment $ _____

Name _____

Company _____

Address _____

City_____ State _____ Country _____ Postal code _____

Email _____

get your conference navigator guide

Think of the last conference you attended...*did you make notes and never look at them again*? If so, you need a Conference Navigator Guide.

The Conference Navigator Guides helps you find more and bigger ideas at the conference, and then shows you how to convert your ideas into actions back at work. The Guides replace the pad of paper you get at a conference with a fun yet serious 60-page idea journal. Each page is designed to encourage participants to listen for ideas and act on them. Pages include:

- Assess your past participation.
- What is a great idea?
- Where do great ideas come from?
- How to pick your workshops.
- Active listening to different types of speakers.
- Active note taking.
- Swapping ideas with others.
- Mingle mingle—how to network.
- Taking the great ideas home.
- Turning ideas into actions.

Plus...30 pages for notes and a place to insert business cards of important contacts people make.

> **"Once in a while a new idea surfaces that makes me wonder...**
>
> **"Why didn't I think of that?"**
>
> George Gendron, editor of *Inc.* Magazine said this about the Conference Navigator Guides. *Inc.* Magazine used the Navigator at all of its conferences in 1998.

Send me a Conference Navigator Guide!

No. of guides _____ × $29.95 = Total $_____

Shipping $2.50 in Australia, $5.00 internationally $_____

(GST inclusive)   Total payment $_____

Send your cheque to:
The Idea Factory, GPO Box 1074J, Melbourne, Victoria, Australia 3001

Name _____

Company _____

Address _____

City _____ State _____ Country _____ Postal code _____

Email _____

wow!

that's a

great
idea!

An ideal corporate gift for your team, customers or suppliers!

This book will give your team, or your customers or suppliers a tremendous resource for finding new and powerful ideas to make their business more innovative and effective.

To order extra copies, use this form or email your request to wow@ideafactory.com.au Individual orders are $29.95 (plus shipping of $2.50 within Australia or $5.00 internationally).

For a larger order, you will receive a major discount

- For 5–10 copies, your investment is $25.00 per copy (plus $2.50 shipping).
- For 11–25 copies, your investment is $22.50 per copy (plus $5.00 shipping). You also receive for FREE, a copy of Ed Bernacki's Conference Navigator Guide, a $29.95 value.
- For 26 or more, your investment is $20.00 per copy (plus $8.00 shipping). Your also receive for FREE, a copy of Ed Bernacki's Conference Navigator Guide, a $29.95 value plus a set of set of posters to accompany the book, a $39.95 value.
- For orders over 100 books, email wow@ideafactory.com.au

Send me more wow! that's a great idea! books!

Send this page and your cheque to:
The Idea Factory, GPO Box 1074J, Melbourne, Victoria, Australia 3001.
(If you prefer use a separate sheet of paper.)

No. of books _____ × cost per book _____ = Total $ _____

(GST inclusive)   Shipping $ _____

                                                               Total payment $ _____

Name _____

Company _____

Address _____

City_____ State _____ Country _____ Postal code _____

Email _____

get your conference navigator guide

Think of the last conference you attended...*did you make notes and never look at them again?* If so, you need a Conference Navigator Guide.

The Conference Navigator Guides helps you find more and bigger ideas at the conference, and then shows you how to convert your ideas into actions back at work. The Guides replace the pad of paper you get at a conference with a fun yet serious 60-page idea journal. Each page is designed to encourage participants to listen for ideas and act on them. Pages include:

"Once in a while a new idea surfaces that makes me wonder...

"Why didn't I think of that?"

George Gendron, editor of *Inc.* Magazine said this about the Conference Navigator Guides. *Inc.* Magazine used the Navigator at all of its conferences in 1998.

- Assess your past participation.
- What is a great idea?
- Where do great ideas come from?
- How to pick your workshops.
- Active listening to different types of speakers.
- Active note taking.
- Swapping ideas with others.
- Mingle mingle—how to network.
- Taking the great ideas home.
- Turning ideas into actions.

Plus...30 pages for notes and a place to insert business cards of important contacts people make.

Send me a Conference Navigator Guide!

No. of guides _____ × $29.95 = Total $_____

Shipping $2.50 in Australia, $5.00 internationally $_____

(GST inclusive)   Total payment $_____

Send your cheque to:
The Idea Factory, GPO Box 1074J, Melbourne, Victoria, Australia 3001

Name _____

Company _____

Address _____

City _____ State _____ Country _____ Postal code _____

Email _____

wow!

that's a

great idea!

An ideal corporate gift for your team, customers or suppliers!

This book will give your team, or your customers or suppliers a tremendous resource for finding new and powerful ideas to make their business more innovative and effective.

To order extra copies, use this form or email your request to wow@ideafactory.com.au Individual orders are $29.95 (plus shipping of $2.50 within Australia or $5.00 internationally).

For a larger order, you will receive a major discount

- For 5–10 copies, your investment is $25.00 per copy (plus $2.50 shipping).
- For 11–25 copies, your investment is $22.50 per copy (plus $5.00 shipping). You also receive for FREE, a copy of Ed Bernacki's Conference Navigator Guide, a $29.95 value.
- For 26 or more, your investment is $20.00 per copy (plus $8.00 shipping). Your also receive for FREE, a copy of Ed Bernacki's Conference Navigator Guide, a $29.95 value plus a set of set of posters to accompany the book, a $39.95 value.
- For orders over 100 books, email wow@ideafactory.com.au

Send me more wow! that's a great idea! books!

Send this page and your cheque to:
The Idea Factory, GPO Box 1074J, Melbourne, Victoria, Australia 3001.
(If you prefer use a separate sheet of paper.)

No. of books _____ × cost per book _____ = Total $_____

(GST inclusive)   Shipping $_____

                                                Total payment $_____

Name _____

Company _____

Address _____

City_____ State _____ Country _____ Postal code _____

Email _____